Refresh

A **Wellness** Devotional for the **Whole** Christian Life

Jo Acharya

Images by Dan Acharya

malcolm down

PUBLISHING

First published 2021 by Malcolm Down Publishing Ltd
www.malcolmdown.co.uk
Registered Office: Welwyn Garden City, England

British Library Cataloguing in Publication Data
A catalogue record for this book is available from the British Library.

ISBN 978-1-915046-02-4

Cover design by Esther Kotecha
Art direction by Sarah Grace

Printed in the UK

What others are saying about *Refresh* . . .

Good habits really help us become resilient. When we're under pressure, those habits can keep us afloat and stop us from crashing. Resources like *Refresh* enable us to go on a journey of developing those habits which are crucial for our wellbeing.

Patrick Regan OBE, *co-founder and CEO of Kintsugi Hope; author of* When Faith Gets Shaken *and* Bouncing Forwards

So many of us find it difficult to find the time and energy to spend time exploring scripture and allowing it to feed our souls. As a person with long-term illness, I have found that *Refresh* is a collection of reflections that gives me space to be with God within my daily pain. It is a delight: gentle, honest, and hopeful.

It's a devotional with a heart for wellbeing, and it admits the pain and grief in life while pointing us towards the light and truth to be found in Jesus. The reflections can be taken at differing paces, with flexibility for those of us who struggle.

With content based around subjects like rest, belonging, struggle and celebration, it is a well-rounded and beautifully presented book, with images that will soothe your soul and words that will console and nourish you at every level. Highly recommended.

Liz Carter, *author of* Catching Contentment: how to be holy satisfied *and* Treasure in Dark Places

My wife Caz and I were thrilled when Jo gave us an early copy of *Refresh* to work through. Not only was this a book which would bless us, but we immediately knew it would be such a useful tool for discipleship in the local church. Beautifully presented, thoughtfully written, and scripturally rooted, *Refresh* is going to serve individuals and groups in their growth as Christ followers.

Of course, behind every book is an author, and even more than the book, I am so confident to endorse Jo. Her character, love for Jesus and his people, and the lifetime of grappling with her faith which has gone into shaping the text are elements that shine through in her writing.

Steve Alliston, *pastor of Crawley Community Church*

For Ruth, who embraced life with honesty, courage and grace. She lived the message of this book far better than I can write it.

Contents

Healthy Life

Healthy Heart

Healthy Faith

Introduction

Welcome! Wherever you're starting from, we hope that *Refresh* will be a gentle companion on your Christian journey.

If you're looking for a flexible way to fit time with God into your busy life, *Refresh* is for you. It's designed to fit around your schedule, and to help you find space to slow down and reflect. The undated format means you can take breaks when you need to and pick up again where you left off. No pressure, no guilt.

If you're feeling weighed down, weary or far from God, *Refresh* is for you. The devotionals are short and accessible, designed to meet you where you are. We hope you'll find encouragement to be real with God and strength for when the journey is hard.

If you believe in Jesus but aren't sure what that means for your life, *Refresh* is for you. You'll discover that God has a lot to say about how to live a healthy life, and that he wants to be involved in yours! We also recommend joining a church if you can, or meeting with other Christians to worship God and learn more about him.

If you're struggling with your physical or mental health, *Refresh* is for you. The teaching is sensitive to different life circumstances and challenges, and the flexible format provides an easy, low-energy way to engage with God at your own pace.

Each topic will encourage you to think about a different area of your life. The questions and weekly reflections may help you work towards positive changes, and they might also reveal areas where you could benefit from some extra support – perhaps from a loved one, pastor, doctor or therapist. Appropriate medication, counselling, CBT (cognitive behavioural therapy) and arts therapies are all God-given tools that can often improve wellbeing.

How to Use this Book

Each week's content includes:

- a Bible passage and short discussion about an aspect of the current topic

- three questions to help you think and pray about how this might relate to your life

- weekly reflections to help you look back on your week and think about how you're doing personally

- two optional extra Bible passages to help you dig deeper if you'd like to (found at the end of each topic)

You can split each week into as many sessions as you like. Here are some suggestions to get you started, but feel free to experiment and create your own routine.

1 session per week:
Weekend: this week's weekly reflections and next week's Bible passage, discussion and questions

3 sessions per week:
Session 1 – Bible passage and discussion
Session 2 – questions
Session 3 – weekly reflections

Daily sessions:

Monday	–	Bible passage and discussion
Tuesday	–	question 1
Wednesday	–	question 2
Thursday	–	question 3
Friday	–	extra Bible passage 1
Saturday	–	extra Bible passage 2
Sunday	–	weekly reflections

Each topic lasts four weeks. At the end of each topic there's a chance to reflect on what you've learned, as well as some suggested further resources.

Refresh can be quick and simple, or a jumping off point for further Bible study and prayer. Together, the thirteen topics paint a picture of a healthy life, heart and faith: wellbeing as God designed it.

Notes on the Content

The Bible passages are taken from the New International Version (NIV) Anglicised edition unless otherwise indicated. References in brackets are in the format 'Book Chapter: Verses' (e.g. Genesis 1:1-2). References that come from that week's Bible passage include only the verses (v1-2) or the chapter and verses (1:1-2)

The questions are prompts to help you begin to think and pray about what you've been reading. There is blank space provided for you to write or draw your answers. You may have other thoughts to add. Ask God to guide you as you work through them.

Thinking about some of the questions may bring up strong feelings. If a question is difficult or painful to think about, feel free to skip it, or perhaps talk and pray about it with someone you trust. If several of the questions in a topic are hard for you to think about, this may be a sign that you need some extra support to explore how this topic applies to your own life.

The further resources at the end of each topic are a mixture of books, music, talks and more. They are from a variety of Christian traditions and viewpoints, so they have differing beliefs about some areas of faith. We hope they will help you think more deeply about each topic by looking at the Bible's teaching from different perspectives.

Ready to Begin . . .

We hope that the words and images in this book will help you to grow in your faith, to get to know God better and to experience his love for you more fully. We pray that you will find greater freedom and healing as you spend time with him.

> *Learn from me, for I am gentle and humble in heart,*
> *and you will find rest for your souls.*
>
> Jesus, Matthew 11:29

Rest

Most of us find it difficult to rest. There's always more to do, and our culture expects us to never switch off. But we all need rest. It is a blessing that God calls us to welcome and enjoy.

Rest #1

> *In six days the Lord made the heavens and the earth,*
> *the sea, and all that is in them, but he rested on the*
> *seventh day. Therefore the Lord blessed the*
> *Sabbath day and made it holy.*
>
> Exodus 20:11

Read: Exodus 20:8-11

The Israelites had been slaves in Egypt for over 200 years. Then God miraculously rescued them and brought them out into the desert. They had been surrounded by the Egyptian culture and religion, and they'd got used to it. They had forgotten how to follow their own God.

So God's first task once he had freed his people was to make them into a community of faith who would live his way. He had created them, and he knew what was best for them. He built into their new lifestyle a rhythm of work and rest, ending each week with a holy 'Sabbath'. On the Sabbath, all work would stop. The people would spend the whole day worshipping God, relaxing and enjoying time together.

As Christians, we are not commanded to keep the Sabbath in the same way as the Israelites (Colossians 2:16). But finding a balance between work and rest is still important. For some of us, setting aside one day each week for rest creates a healthy routine. For others, taking smaller chunks of time during the week might work better.

However we choose to do it, the Bible encourages us to welcome rest as a generous gift from the God who loves us. He knows what we need, and he modelled this rhythm for us in the story of creation.

> This week, think about how you balance work and rest, and try to make some changes if you need to.

- How can you build rest periods into your week?

- Which works better for you, a whole day off, or smaller chunks of rest time during the week?

- What are the challenges for you in keeping a healthy work/rest balance?

*In six days the Lord made the heavens and the earth, the sea,
and all that is in them, but he rested on the seventh day.
Therefore the Lord blessed the Sabbath day and made it holy.*

Exodus 20:11

Weekly Reflections

Good things

Hard things

General mood

How have I rested?

What help do I need?

What have I worried about?

Who can I ask for help?

What has calmed me down?

	🙂	😐	🙁
Eating	🙂	😐	🙁
Sleep	🙂	😐	🙁
Exercise	🙂	😐	🙁

Prayer for next week

Rest #2

> *In peace I will lie down and sleep, for you alone,*
> *LORD, make me dwell in safety.*
>
> Psalm 4:8

Read: Psalm 4

David was on the run when he wrote Psalm 4. God had chosen him to be the next king of Israel, and Saul, the current king, was jealous and angry. Saul had sent soldiers to kill David, so his life was in great danger.

In our busy world it can be hard to make rest a priority. There always seems to be more to do. We might feel that if we stop for a moment, we'll lose control of all the balls we're trying to juggle. Maybe we're worried that without our constant input things won't get done, or at least not properly. Or perhaps we're fearful of the anxious thoughts that could take over our minds if we don't keep busy.

Whatever situation we're in, our bodies and minds do need regular rest to function well. David could have forced himself to stay awake in case his enemies attacked. Instead, he saw his need for sleep as an opportunity to remind himself of who was really in control. He trusted God to keep him safe while he slept.

Rest can be an act of faith in God. It's a way of declaring that it's him, not us, who keeps the world turning. And it's a regular chance to freely give up control and entrust our cares to him.

This week, try to see rest as a chance to freely give up control and entrust your cares to God.

- Are there any worries or fears that keep you from resting well?

- How do you feel about giving up control? Do you want to resist, or is it a relief?

- Does rest feel different when you look at it this way?

In peace I will lie down and sleep, for you alone,
LORD, make me dwell in safety.

Psalm 4:8

Weekly Reflections

Good things

Hard things

Main focus

How has it felt to rest?

What am I grateful for?

What have I done well?

Who can I thank?

What can I do better?

Eating	🙂	😐	☹️
Sleep	🙂	😐	☹️
Exercise	🙂	😐	☹️

Prayer for next week

Rest #3

week beginning _____

> *[Jesus said to his disciples], 'Come with me by yourselves to a quiet place and get some rest.'*
>
> Mark 6:31

Read: Mark 6:30-46

At every stage of life, there are demands on our time. Those demands don't always stop when we need to rest. So how do we carve out quality rest time in the midst of busyness, or even chaos?

Jesus's later life was full of constant pressure. Huge crowds followed him everywhere he went, eager to hear his teachings and receive healing. His disciples kept making mistakes and needing correction. And the religious leaders wanted him dead! But even in these busy and stressful times, Jesus carefully guarded his time alone. He knew he needed to recharge and refocus, especially with prayer and sleep.

Sometimes life does force us to be flexible. In this passage, Jesus put off resting so he could meet the needs of the crowd (v30-34). Even so, he took the next opportunity to go away by himself for some much-needed alone time (v45-46).

Our need for rest increases when the physical, mental or emotional demands on us are high. At those times it's even more important to recognise the signs that we need a break.

Life doesn't always go according to plan. There are times when a task can't wait, or someone needs us right away. But like Jesus, we must be determined and creative in finding ways to carve out the breathing space we need.

This week, try to notice the signs that you need a break, and find creative ways to meet that need.

- What are the biggest demands on your time and energy right now?

- What are some of the signs that warn you when you need a break?

- How can you guard your rest time? Can you schedule it, or do you need to be flexible?

[Jesus said to his disciples], 'Come with me by yourselves to a quiet place and get some rest.'

Mark 6:31

Weekly Reflections

Good things

Hard things

General mood

How have I found creative ways to rest?

What do I need to talk about?

How have I blessed others?

Who can I talk with?

How have others blessed me?

Eating	☺	☺	☹
Sleep	☺	☺	☹
Exercise	☺	☺	☹

Prayer for next week

Rest #4 week beginning _____

> *Come to me, all you who are weary and burdened,*
> *and I will give you rest.*
>
> Matthew 11:28

Read: Matthew 11:25-30

Followers of Jesus are not promised an easy time. On almost every page of the Bible we read about people whose lives were anything but quiet and peaceful. Some were given big jobs to do. Others had to deal with difficult people and situations. Many suffered great pain and loss.

What Jesus offers us is not a quiet, peaceful life, but a quiet, peaceful soul. That's a kind of rest that doesn't depend on our circumstances. It comes from spending time with him, slowing down and being still in his presence.

A soul at rest knows that we have been saved by grace, not by our own effort (Ephesians 2:8-9). A soul at rest knows that we can rely on God's strength to do all he asks us to do (Philippians 4:13). A soul at rest knows that nothing can separate us from God's love for us (Romans 8:38-39).

If anything in life is weighing us down or wearing us out, Jesus encourages us to bring it to him. Each day we can choose to release the worries that aren't ours to carry. Each day we can let him take the weight of the heavy burdens that we've struggled with for so long. As we rest in his gentle presence, he refreshes us with strength and energy for the work he's given us to do.

> This week, bring your burdens to Jesus.

- What burdens are you carrying? Do they come from your circumstances, or from others' expectations, or your own?

- Which burdens can you let go of completely? Which ones do you need Jesus's strength to bear?

- Which Bible verses give peace and rest to your soul?

Come to me, all you who are weary and burdened,
and I will give you rest.

Matthew 11:28

Weekly Reflections

Good things

Hard things

Main focus

What has refreshed my soul?

What am I proud of?

How have I spoken to myself?

Who can I celebrate with?

What has encouraged me?

Eating	☺	😐	☹
Sleep	☺	😐	☹
Exercise	☺	😐	☹

Prayer for next week

Rest Reflections

3-word summary

-
-
-

Verse to remember

What have I found challenging?

What have I found rewarding?

Favourite insight

What will I carry forward?

Rest prayer

Rest Optional Extra Bible Passages

Rest #1

- Genesis 1:1 – 2:3
  God creates the world and rests on the seventh day

- Leviticus 25:1-22
  Laws about rest for people, animals and the earth

Rest #3

- Psalm 121
  God does not get tired or sleep, and he is always watching over us

- Luke 12:22-34
  Encouragement to trust God with all things

Rest #2

- Job 38:4-21
  God's power compared to ours – he is in control

- Psalm 23
  Resting in God's faithful care

Rest #4

- Isaiah 55:1-7
  Encouragement to rest in God's presence

- Hebrews 3:7 – 4:16
  We must strive to enter God's rest

Rest Further Resources

- **Book:** *The Ruthless Elimination of Hurry: how to stay emotionally healthy and spiritually alive in the chaos of the modern world* by John Mark Comer
  Written in a conversational tone, with wise principles for slowing down and making room for God in busy lives.

- **Music:** *Still* (volume 1) by Rivers and Robots
  A relaxing hour of instrumental worship, including new arrangements of familiar songs. Each volume in the Still series is by a different artist, with their own musical style.

- **Colouring Book:** *Images of Grace* by Jacqui Grace
  Each page centres around a Bible verse, charmingly illustrated with a scene from everyday life. The *Images of . . .* series is lovely – an easy way to rest and memorise encouraging verses at the same time!

Your Notes

Nourish

Caring for ourselves includes looking after our physical needs. Many of us have complicated relationships with our bodies, but they are an important part of us, created and loved by God.

Nourish #1 week beginning _____

> *For you created my inmost being; you knit me together in my mother's womb. I praise you because I am fearfully and wonderfully made.*
>
> Psalm 139:13-14

Read: Psalm 139:1-18

Most of us would change something about our bodies if we could. It can be hard to live with bodies that don't work as they should or don't look as we would like them to. We may feel disconnected from our physical selves, as if they are separate from us. Some of us use our bodies to express our creativity, or train them to achieve amazing goals. Others of us may feel imprisoned, controlled or even attacked by bodies that limit us or cause us pain. Our bodies can bring up powerful feelings, from gratitude and wonder to frustration or shame. And they often play an important part in the stories of our lives.

The Bible tells us that we are not just spiritual beings. We are also physical creatures made for a physical world (Genesis 2:7). This world is damaged in many ways. The bodies we live in during our time on earth are imperfect, and they will one day decay and die. But we can still see God's good, loving design in movement, touch, language, taste, thinking and laughter. We experience all the ordinary and amazing moments of our lives through our frail but wonderful bodies.

To be 'fearfully' made means to be created with great honour and respect. God forms our bodies with skilled hands, breathes his life and love into them, and calls his creation good.

> This week, try to honour and respect your body as God's good creation.

- How would you describe your feelings towards your body? Where do these come from?

- Do you think of your body as an essential part of you, or as something separate from your real self?

- Where can you see God's good design within your body, and in the things it allows you to do?

For you created my inmost being; you knit me together in my mother's womb. I praise you because I am fearfully and wonderfully made.

Psalm 139:13-14

Weekly Reflections

Good things	Hard things	General mood

How have I honoured my body?

What help do I need?

What have I worried about?

Who can I ask for help?

What has calmed me down?

	🙂	😐	☹️
Eating			
Sleep			
Exercise			

Prayer for next week

Nourish #2 week beginning _____

> *All at once an angel touched him and said,*
> *'Get up and eat.'*
>
> 1 Kings 19:5

Read: 1 Kings 19:1-8

Elijah was on a mission to win the wayward people of Israel back to faith in God. In a showdown with the prophets of the false god Baal, Elijah had called down fire from heaven. This proved that his God was the only true God. But instead of winning the nation back, this had made the king furious. Now Elijah was running for his life. This great man had lost hope, and he was ready to give up. He even prayed for death.

When we are struggling emotionally, there are many things that can help. Thinking about positive things, finding comfort in calming activities and seeking encouragement from friends all play an important role. But it's easy to forget that our most basic needs are physical. When Elijah was weary and depressed, God knew what he needed. Sleep and food restored his spirit and gave him energy to continue his mission. For us, sleep, food and exercise all help to form a healthy lifestyle, not just for our bodies but also our minds.

Our bodies are designed to give us signals like hunger and tiredness. These signals are a useful guide if they are working well, but they can go wrong. And some of us live with incurable symptoms or pain – if we can't act on our body's signals, it may not be helpful to focus too much on them. It's important to know our own bodies, so that we can treat them well and meet their needs as best we can.

> This week, pay attention to your body's signals and think about how you respond to your physical needs.

- What are your strategies when you're struggling emotionally? Do your physical needs play a part?

- How well do you know your body? Are the signals it gives you helpful?

- What are some of the ways you can treat your body well and meet its needs?

All at once an angel touched him and said,
'Get up and eat.'

1 Kings 19:5

Weekly Reflections

Good things

Hard things

Main focus

How have I looked after my physical needs?

What am I grateful for?

What have I done well?

Who can I thank?

What can I do better?

	🙂	😐	☹️
Eating	🙂	😐	☹️
Sleep	🙂	😐	☹️
Exercise	🙂	😐	☹️

Prayer for next week

Nourish #3 week beginning_____

> *The Word became flesh and made his dwelling among us. We have seen his glory, the glory of the one and only Son, who came from the Father.*
>
> John 1:14

Read: John 1:1-18

The greatest honour our creator could have given us was to become human himself and live in our world in a physical body. Jesus was born as a baby. He learned to speak and walk. He ate, drank and slept. He respected his body's limitations and treated it with care. For thirty-three years the maker of the universe experienced what it was like to live in a fragile human body. Like ours, his body could sweat, get dirty and even bleed. At the end of his earthly life, Jesus's body was beaten, pierced and broken. He felt deeply the physical, mental and spiritual effects of his suffering.

Most of us live at least part of our lives with damaged bodies. It's comforting that we have a God who knows what it's like to feel pain and to be weary. It also gives us hope to know that after his resurrection, Jesus's body was transformed. His new body was no longer limited by the laws of nature, although he still bore the scars of his former life (John 20:26-27). Our earthly bodies are frail, but we look forward to glorious new bodies, which will be eternal (2 Corinthians 5:1).

The humanity of Jesus is God's seal of approval on the world he created, including our physical bodies. He is willing to meet us in the joy and in the mess, and to take our sufferings upon himself. Because God made himself one of us, we can understand both him and ourselves more clearly.

> This week, think about Jesus's humanity and what this means to you.

- What does Jesus's humanity show you about God? What does it show you about yourself?

- In what ways might Jesus have shared your particular joys and struggles during his earthly life?

- Can you imagine how your eternal body will be different to your earthly one? How might it be similar?

The Word became flesh and made his dwelling among us.
We have seen his glory, the glory of the one and only Son,
who came from the Father.

John 1:14

Weekly Reflections

Good things	Hard things	General mood

How have I related to Jesus in his humanity?

What do I need to talk about?

How have I blessed others?

Who can I talk with?

How have others blessed me?

Eating	🙂	😐	☹️
Sleep	🙂	😐	☹️
Exercise	🙂	😐	☹️

Prayer for next week

Nourish #4 week beginning _____

> *Do you not know that your bodies are temples*
> *of the Holy Spirit, who is in you?...*
> *Therefore honour God with your bodies.*
>
> 1 Corinthians 6:19-20

Read: 1 Corinthians 6:12-20

The church in Corinth was founded by the apostle Paul, but leading them proved to be a real challenge. In his letters to this church, Paul had to address deep-rooted patterns of pride, division and sinful behaviour. But in correcting them, he gave us this wonderful image of our bodies as temples of the Holy Spirit himself – as God's home on earth.

In Exodus chapters 25 to 26 God told the Israelites to build him a movable home, called a tabernacle. This was so he could live with his people as they wandered through the desert. According to God's detailed instructions, the tabernacle was built by skilled workers from the most precious materials available. Later, when they came into their own land, the Israelites built him a new home – a glorious temple made from even more lavish materials. But from the start, God's ultimate plan was to live not just alongside us, but within us. He chooses to make his home in our bodies, which to him are more wonderful than even the most magnificent building.

The tabernacle and the temple were holy – set apart for God. Now, our own bodies have been set apart for God and made holy by his presence. Paul encourages us to offer them to him as living sacrifices (Romans 12:1), using our thoughts, words and actions to honour the God who lives within us.

This week, try to think of your body as a temple of the Holy Spirit, his home on earth.

- How does it affect your feelings towards your body to know that God himself has chosen to live within it?

- Thinking of yourself as a temple, what are some of the 'precious materials' God has used to create you?

- What are some ways you can honour God with your body (thoughts, words and actions)?

Do you not know that your bodies are temples
of the Holy Spirit, who is in you?…
Therefore honour God with your bodies.

1 Corinthians 6:19-20

Weekly Reflections

Good things	Hard things	Main focus

How have I honoured God with my body?

What am I proud of?

How have I spoken to myself?

Who can I celebrate with?

What has encouraged me?

	🙂	😐	☹️
Eating			
Sleep			
Exercise			

Prayer for next week

Nourish Reflections

3-word summary

-
-
-

Verse to remember

What have I found challenging?

What have I found rewarding?

Favourite insight

What will I carry forward?

Nourish prayer

Nourish Optional Extra Bible Passages

Nourish #1

- Psalm 8

  God has given humans dignity and worth

- Song of Songs 4:1-7, 5:10-16

  Praise for the beauty of the human body

Nourish #3

- Luke 2:1-20

  Jesus's birth as a human baby

- 2 Corinthians 4:7 – 5:10

  Our bodies gradually decay, but inwardly we are being renewed

Nourish #2

- Exodus 16

  God provides food for the Israelites in the desert

- Colossians 2:16-23

  God has no special rules about food

Nourish #4

- Exodus 25 – 26

  The most precious materials used to build God's tabernacle

- Romans 11:33 – 12:21

  Our bodies are a living sacrifice to God

Nourish Further Resources

- **Book:** *Embracing the Body: finding God in our flesh and bone* by Tara M. Owens

  A sensitive guide to relating positively to our bodies, with practical exercises and a spiritual focus.

- **Blog:** *'Body B Loved'* by Nicole Mesita and others

  Dozens of wise, healing articles written by Christian dietitians who want to help others develop healthy relationships with food and their bodies, rather than focusing on weight loss. Find it at bodybloved.com/home.

- **Book (men***):** *Reset: living a grace-paced life in a burnout culture* by David Murray

  Book (women): *Refresh: embracing a grace-paced life in a world of endless demands* by Shona and David Murray

  Clear, helpful advice on all aspects of looking after our bodies and minds well, and living within healthy limits.

Your Notes

Belong

Loneliness is one of the hardest things for a human being to deal with. Even though relationships can be difficult, we are made to live together in honest, messy, life-giving community.

Belong #1 week beginning _____

> *The LORD God said, 'It is not good for the man to be alone. I will make a helper suitable for him.'*
>
> Genesis 2:18

Read: Genesis 2:15-24

Adam was the first man, created from the earth by God's own hand. He lived in a new and beautiful world, and enjoyed a wonderful, perfect friendship with God. His relationship with creation was also joyful and unspoiled. Yet God looked at Adam and saw that there was something 'not good' in Adam's life. In God's own words, Adam was alone.

Adam needed a partner to help him live out his calling as a human made in God's image. But his relationships were unequal. God was far above him, and the animals were under his rule. God's creation of Eve shows us that each human is designed to live in community with other humans. We are to be a team of equals who can understand, support and work with each other. When Adam saw Eve, he immediately recognised someone who was like himself – a suitable helper, and a true partner. Adam was no longer alone.

Like Adam, we need helpers who are suitable for us. We need to share the experience of being human and walk with others like us along the path of life. We know that the journey of relationship is not always smooth. Our differences and similarities are often frustrating. We can be hurt, and we can hurt those we love. But, flawed as we all are, only healthy community has the power to draw us out of isolation and into the God-given shelter of belonging.

This week, think about how your experience of community compares to God's intentions for us.

- Do you ever feel lonely? How do you deal with this?

- Which people in your life are you grateful for? How have they been 'suitable helpers' for you?

- What has your experience of community been like? What are some of the benefits and challenges?

The LORD God said, 'It is not good for the man to be alone.
I will make a helper suitable for him.'

Genesis 2:18

Weekly Reflections

Good things	Hard things	General mood

How have I enjoyed community with other people?

What help do I need?

What have I worried about?

Who can I ask for help?

What has calmed me down?

Eating	☺	😐	☹
Sleep	☺	😐	☹
Exercise	☺	😐	☹

Prayer for next week

Belong #2   week beginning _____

> *Therefore, as God's chosen people, holy and dearly loved, clothe yourselves with compassion, kindness, humility, gentleness and patience.*
>
> Colossians 3:12

Read: Colossians 3:5-17

The New Testament letters are full of commands to love one other. It seems that this was something the early Christians struggled with as much as we often do! Relationships are complicated, and it takes work to keep them healthy.

In this picture, Paul spoke of 'taking off' and 'putting on' different ways of relating to one another, like items of clothing. He knew that kindness and gentleness don't always come naturally, especially if we've learned unhealthy ways of relating from parents or friends. To begin with, choosing to be patient with someone who annoys us might feel stiff and awkward, like walking in a new pair of shoes. But as we choose to 'wear' these godly attitudes each day, they become more and more comfortable. As Christians we're being changed by the Holy Spirit to make us more like Jesus and our new, *true* selves (v10). Our part in this is an active choice to 'put on' qualities that reflect God's heart.

Real love does take courage. It means speaking up when our friends are in the wrong, and allowing them to do the same for us. It means apologising and forgiving. There are times, too, when a relationship becomes so harmful that it needs to end (2 Timothy 3:1-9). But choosing to clothe ourselves in love and forgiveness, even from a distance if necessary, can help us heal and find freedom from the wounds of the past.

> This week, try to clothe yourself in godly qualities as you live in relationship with others.

- What are your natural attitudes in your relationships? What qualities do you have to actively 'put on'?

- How good are you at giving correction where it's needed? How good are you at accepting it from others?

- How can we put on love and forgiveness 'from a distance' after a difficult relationship has ended?

*Therefore, as God's chosen people, holy and dearly
loved, clothe yourselves with compassion, kindness,
humility, gentleness and patience.*

Colossians 3:12

Weekly Reflections

Good things	Hard things	Main focus

How have I 'put on' godly qualities?

What am I grateful for?

What have I done well?

Who can I thank?

What can I do better?

Eating	:)	:|	:(
Sleep	:)	:|	:(
Exercise	:)	:|	:(

Prayer for next week

Belong #3 week beginning _____

> *Ruth replied, 'Don't urge me to leave you ...*
> *Where you go I will go, and where you stay I will stay.*
> *Your people will be my people and your God my God.'*
>
> ### Ruth 1:16

Read: Ruth 1:1-18

Naomi had lost everything. Crushed by grief, she tried to cut off ties with those who loved her. Even though she needed community more than ever, she wanted only to be left alone. But Ruth would not be pushed away. Their story shows the power of loyal friendship to restore broken lives.

It's not easy to walk lightly with someone who is suffering. Other people's pain can make us feel uneasy and helpless. We may feel an urge to run away, or to give too much and risk emotional burnout. To take on the role of Ruth means accepting that we cannot fix what's wrong, and staying in the relationship anyway. A faithful friend is a healing presence.

It can be challenging to support those in pain. But many of us still feel much more comfortable caring for others than accepting our own need for help. It's hard to be Naomi. When we're struggling, our first instinct is often to isolate ourselves. We may be afraid to admit weakness. Perhaps we think no one will understand what we're going through. Like Naomi, we might even feel that everyone else is better off without us. But embracing community means being vulnerable and open.

Sometimes we take the role of the helper, and at other times we allow ourselves to be helped. Through mutual trust and support, we can all flourish.

> This week, think about the ways you help others and the areas where you need help.

- Do you see yourself more as a helper or as someone who needs help? How comfortable are you with this?

- How can you protect yourself from emotional burnout when supporting others? .

- How do you feel about accepting help from others? Are there areas where this is harder or easier?

Ruth replied, 'Don't urge me to leave you …
Where you go I will go, and where you stay I will stay.
Your people will be my people and your God my God.'

Ruth 1:16

Weekly Reflections

Good things

Hard things

General mood

How have I given and accepted help?

What do I need to talk about?

How have I blessed others?

Who can I talk with?

How have others blessed me?

Eating	☺	😐	☹
Sleep	☺	😐	☹
Exercise	☺	😐	☹

Prayer for next week

Belong #4   week beginning _____

> *But you are a chosen people, a royal priesthood,*
> *a holy nation … Once you were not a people,*
> *but now you are the people of God.*
>
> 1 Peter 2:9-10

Read: 1 Peter 2:4-17

In the early days of the Church, new Christians who had nothing else in common came together around their shared faith in Jesus. For rich and poor people, slaves and slave owners, Jews and Gentiles (non-Jews), shaping this new community was sometimes a challenge. At the same time they were often being mistreated because of their faith. In this letter the apostle Peter urged his readers to hold on to their unity in Jesus, and stand strong as the people of God.

The Bible's model for Christian living is to be in community with other believers. The world is full of distractions and difficulties that try to pull us away from Jesus. On our own, it's hard to stay on the right path. Meeting together encourages and strengthens us, as well as binding us closer together in love for God and each other.

Christian community is far more than just going to church on Sundays. It's caring for each other, and supporting each other to grow in relationship with God. That can happen in a group of a hundred people, or just two. But it's not always easy. Some of us have been hurt by other Christians and even by churches.

Wherever there are human beings, we will always find sin. Even so, the cure for harmful community is healthy community, not isolation. Only in the presence of God's people can we fully take our place in his holy nation.

This week, think about what being part of the Church means to you.

- How has meeting with other Christians encouraged and strengthened you in your faith?

- What does it mean to think of the Church as a 'holy nation'?

- What should unity among Christians look like? Where can you see this kind of unity?

But you are a chosen people, a royal priesthood,
a holy nation ... Once you were not a people,
but now you are the people of God.

1 Peter 2:9-10

Weekly Reflections

Good things

Hard things

Main focus

How have I taken part in Christian community?

What am I proud of?

How have I spoken to myself?

Who can I celebrate with?

What has encouraged me?

Eating	☺	😐	☹
Sleep	☺	😐	☹
Exercise	☺	😐	☹

Prayer for next week

Belong Reflections

3-word summary

-
-
-

Verse to remember

What have I found challenging?

What have I found rewarding?

Favourite insight

What will I carry forward?

Belong prayer

Belong Optional Extra Bible Passages

Belong #1

- Ecclesiastes 4:7-12
  People are strongest in community with others

- 1 Samuel 18:1-4, 20:1-42
  David and Jonathan's friendship

Belong #3

- Matthew 25:31-46
  What we do for each other, we do for Jesus

- Exodus 18:7-27
  Jethro advises Moses to share his work with a team

Belong #2

- 1 Corinthians 13
  God's definition of love

- Proverbs 27:6, 17; 28:23
  Challenging each other within friendships

Belong #4

- John 17:6-25
  Jesus prays for unity among his followers

- Psalm 133
  God wants Christians to be united in love

Belong Further Resources

- **Book:** *Messy, Beautiful Friendship: finding and nurturing deep and lasting relationships* by Christine Hoover
  Friendly and honest, with personal stories and practical advice. Written for women, but relevant to men too. Hoover also recorded a series of interviews in 2018 for her podcast 'By Faith', which discussed different aspects of friendship. Listen at christinehoover. net/podcast-1/.

- **Video Talks:** *Next Level Relationships* by Woodland Hills Church
  Six sermons on a Christian approach to relationships. Watch on YouTube, or listen at whchurch.org/sermon_series/next-level-relationships/.

- **Book:** *Boundaries: when to say yes, how to say no, to take control of your life* by Dr Henry Cloud and Dr John Townsend
  A helpful guide to setting healthy boundaries in life and relationships.

Your Notes

*Each one of us is unique, and we
all have a part to play in the world.
God calls us to enjoy our gifts and
make everything we do an offering
of worship to him.*

Celebrate #1 week beginning _____

> *God has placed the parts in the body, every one of them, just as he wanted them to be ... You are the body of Christ, and each one of you is a part of it.*
>
> 1 Corinthians 12:18, 27

Read: 1 Corinthians 12:12-27

In one of his most famous pictures, Paul imagined the Church as Jesus's body ('the Body of Christ'). A body has many parts that each have their own role, but are designed to work together. Every part is needed. If any one part is in pain or struggling, it hurts the whole body.

It's easy to look around and compare ourselves to others. Some people's roles are flashy and impressive; others are messy or hidden away. Without even meaning to, we can create a scale of importance in our minds, and place ourselves near the top, or right at the bottom. For those of us who don't feel we have a role at all, it can be hard to see our gifts and the value we bring.

But Paul has encouraging words for those of us who aren't sure where we fit. In our physical bodies, the parts that seem weaker are often the ones we need the most. We look after these parts with great care. The heart and lungs don't look like much, but without them the body dies. The same is true in church, and in life. Every one of us has an important part to play. And playing our part isn't just about finding a job to do. Jesus invites us to bring our whole selves to life in the Body of Christ – to boldly be who we are, and who God has created us to be. He calls us to celebrate our personalities, experiences and gifts – the differences that make us unique.

This week, think about this picture of the Body of Christ, and where you see yourself in it.

- Do you ever compare yourself to others and create a 'scale of importance' in your mind? Where do you place yourself on it?

- If you had to describe yourself as a body part, which part would you choose? Why?

- How do you think of your role in the Body of Christ? Is it the jobs you do, or the person you are?

God has placed the parts in the body, every one of them,
just as he wanted them to be... You are the body of Christ,
and each one of you is a part of it.

1 Corinthians 12:18, 27

Weekly Reflections

Good things

Hard things

General mood

How have I celebrated my gifts?

What help do I need?

What have I worried about?

Who can I ask for help?

What has calmed me down?

Eating ☺ 😐 ☹

Sleep ☺ 😐 ☹

Exercise ☺ 😐 ☹

Prayer for next week

Celebrate #2 week beginning _____

> *And who knows but that you have come to your*
> *royal position for such a time as this?*
>
> Esther 4:14

Read: Esther 2:15-18 and 4:1-16

Esther was the Queen of Persia, but she hadn't chosen this life. She had no power or independence. She wasn't even allowed to see the king unless he called for her, and he hadn't called for her in weeks. Esther was trapped in a lonely place. When she heard that her people were in danger, she felt helpless and afraid. But God was about to use her in the most amazing way. He had a plan to save the Jewish people, and he wanted Esther to be part of it.

The Bible says that God wants to work with each of us to make a difference in our world (Ephesians 2:10). It's easy to think of God using things we enjoy and are good at. In these parts of our lives, we feel healthy and useful. But he wants to use the difficult things too – the places where we feel uncomfortable or powerless. That doesn't mean we have to stay in bad jobs or relationships. But when we can't change a difficult situation, God can still use us and bless us (Genesis 50:20).

Sometimes it's in these hard places that we have the most to give! As Isaiah 61:3 says, where we only see ashes, our Father longs to bless us with a crown of beauty.

God sees every part of our lives, and all the places we find ourselves in. He wants to use it all, and to work everything together for his glory and our good (Romans 8:28). Like Esther, we are all invited to play a part in his glorious plan.

This week, think about how God is using you in each area of your life.

- What does playing a part in God's plan mean to you?

- Which parts of your life do you see God using you in most clearly?

- Are there any areas where you don't expect God to use you? What might it look like if he did?

*And who knows but that you have come to your
royal position for such a time as this?*

Esther 4:14

Weekly Reflections

Good things	Hard things	Main focus

How has God used me to make a difference?

What am I grateful for?

What have I done well?

Who can I thank?

What can I do better?

Eating	☺	😐	☹
Sleep	☺	😐	☹
Exercise	☺	😐	☹

Prayer for next week

Celebrate #3 week beginning _____

> *There is nothing better for people than to be*
> *happy and do good while they live. That each of*
> *them may eat and drink, and find satisfaction*
> *in all their toil – this is the gift of God.*
>
> Ecclesiastes 3:12-13

Read: Ecclesiastes 3:1-13

This famous poetic passage paints a rich picture of human life in all its variety. Life can be hard, frustrating and painful. But it can also be joyful and inspiring. The writer decides that to find happiness in simple, ordinary things is a wonderful gift from God.

At times it can feel like our lives are simple and ordinary. We may think that truly meaningful things only happen once in a while. We can also make the mistake of thinking God only cares about 'religious' activities, like prayer and church services. In fact, God is just as interested in everyday things like work, hobbies and relationships. He has given us all these things to enjoy. Not only that, but he also wants to share it all with us. We can choose to invite God into our daily lives, thank him for the gifts he has given us, and honour him in everything we do (1 Corinthians 10:31, Colossians 3:23-24).

If we look at the everyday things of our lives through God's eyes, the way we think about those things will change. We will start to find value even in the smallest of moments, and notice God's presence with us in the midst of all our daily activities. We'll worship on the school run, at the desk, and in the garden. Our Father is not just a Sunday morning God. He's also a Monday lunchtime and Thursday afternoon God – a God who blesses ordinary things and makes them holy.

> This week, try to look at everyday moments as opportunities to worship God.

- Which of your activities do you think of as the most meaningful? What makes them meaningful?

- What might it look like to invite God into everyday activities and think of them as worship?

- What does it mean to you for God to bless ordinary things and make them holy?

*There is nothing better for people than to be
happy and do good while they live. That each of
them may eat and drink, and find satisfaction
in all their toil – this is the gift of God.*

Ecclesiastes 3:12-13

Weekly Reflections

Good things	Hard things	General mood

How have I worshipped God in my daily activities?

What do I need to talk about?

How have I blessed others?

Who can I talk with?

How have others blessed me?

Eating	🙂	😐	🙁
Sleep	🙂	😐	🙁
Exercise	🙂	😐	🙁

Prayer for next week

Celebrate #4 week beginning _____

> *Everything comes from you, and we have given*
> *you only what comes from your hand.*
>
> 1 Chronicles 29:14

Read: 1 Chronicles 29:1-22

King David had once dreamed of building a wonderful temple to God, but God had told him not to do it. Instead, God wanted him to pass this dream on to his son Solomon (1 Chronicles 22:6-10). Now, David was an old man and it was time for him to hand over his kingdom to Solomon. So David did everything he could to get the temple project off to a flying start. He gave from his own riches and encouraged the people to do the same. When David saw how generous the people had been, he praised God, full of joy. He knew that everything already belonged to God (v11). The people were only giving back what he had first given to them.

Many of us give to our churches. This can be a helpful reminder that everything we have belongs to God. But once we've given God 'his share', many of us see the rest of our money, time and gifts as ours, to use however we like. Others of us think God wants us to give all our time and energy to church activities. But when we do this, we have nothing left for other parts of our lives that are just as important.

We all need God's guidance to make the best use of what he's given to us. When we ask him what he wants us to do with what we have, he is ready to show us. Like David, we can even bring him our dreams. Our offerings to God become precious and wonderful in his hands.

> This week, ask God what he wants you to do with the things he's given you.

- Do you think of your money, time and gifts as things that belong to God, or to you?

- Have you ever asked God to show you what he wants you to do with what you have?

- What is your biggest dream? What would it mean to give that to God?

*Everything comes from you, and we have given
you only what comes from your hand.*

1 Chronicles 29:14

Weekly Reflections

Good things	Hard things	Main focus

When have I asked God to guide me?

What am I proud of?

How have I spoken to myself?

Who can I celebrate with?

What has encouraged me?

Eating	☺	😐	☹
Sleep	☺	😐	☹
Exercise	☺	😐	☹

Prayer for next week

Celebrate Reflections

3-word summary

-
-
-

Verse to remember

What have I found challenging?

What have I found rewarding?

Favourite insight

What will I carry forward?

Celebrate prayer

Celebrate Optional Extra Bible Passages

Celebrate #1

- Ephesians 4:1-16
  The church is a body growing into maturity

- Matthew 5:1-16
  Jesus challenges our ideas of what it means to be blessed

Celebrate #3

- 1 Thessalonians 4:1-12
  God gives honour to an ordinary life

- Proverbs 31:10-31
  Praise for all kinds of everyday things done as worship

Celebrate #2

- Acts 9:1-31
  Paul's conversion and calling

- 1 Corinthians 1:18-31
  God chooses the foolish to shame the wise

Celebrate #4

- Psalm 100
  We belong to God and live to worship him

- Luke 10:38-42
  The importance of following God's leading with our gifts

Celebrate Further Resources

- **Book:** *Faithfulness on the Frontline: making a difference where you are* by Mark Greene

  An easy, inspiring and practical read about how we can invite God into our workplaces, homes and relationships. More resources can be found online at licc.org.uk/about/life/.

- **Blog:** 'My Bible' by the Bible Society

  A collection of stories from ordinary people, sharing how God speaks through the Bible and involves himself in everyday lives. The blog is regularly updated. Find it online at biblesociety.org.uk/latest/mybible.

- **Book:** *Everyday God: the spirit of the ordinary* by Paula Gooder

  Using lessons from the Bible, Gooder shows us the beauty of ordinary things, and of ordinary lives lived with God.

Your Notes

Feel

God made us to feel things. Feelings are good, but they are not meant to control us. Learning how to think about our emotions helps us to respond to them in healthy ways.

Feel #1 week beginning _____

> *Jesus wept. Then the Jews said, 'See how he loved him!'*
>
> John 11:35-36

Read: John 11:17-19, 31-44

Jesus visited Lazarus and his sisters, Mary and Martha, whenever he was nearby – they were among his closest friends. Now Lazarus had died. Even though Jesus knew he was going to bring Lazarus back to life, Mary's sadness affected him deeply. When he saw his friend lying dead in the tomb, he cried.

Feelings are one of the things that make us human. In fact, they are part of what it means to be made in the image of God. In the Bible we see that God himself feels emotions like joy (Zephaniah 3:17), sadness (Jeremiah 14:17-18) and anger (1 Kings 11:9-10). In Jesus we see these even more clearly.

Our feelings and moods come from deep within us. They tell us something about what is in our hearts. So when we think about how we feel, it can help us to understand ourselves better. Some of us have a confusing blur of emotions, and find it hard to tell the difference between them. Others of us may not think we have emotions at all. We might think it's best to just ignore how we feel, and work things out logically. But if we don't know what we're feeling, it can be hard to understand how we behave and why we react in the ways we do. Our feelings and moods are an important, God-given tool. Learning to notice them and respond to them wisely can help us make good choices in our lives and relationships.

This week, try to notice your emotions and think about what they are telling you.

- What do you think about emotions? Do you see them as good, bad, helpful or unhelpful?

- What part do emotions play in your decision making? Do you think of yourself as a 'feeler' or a 'logical thinker', or a mixture of both?

- If you kept a record of your feelings and moods each day, which ones would come up most often? What situations would they be connected with?

Jesus wept. Then the Jews said, 'See how he loved him!'

John 11:35-36

Weekly Reflections

Good things	Hard things	General mood

When have I noticed my emotions?

What help do I need?

What have I worried about?

Who can I ask for help?

What has calmed me down?

	🙂	😐	🙁
Eating			
Sleep			
Exercise			

Prayer for next week

Feel #2

> *Trust in the LORD with all your heart and*
> *lean not on your own understanding.*
>
> Proverbs 3:5

Read: Proverbs 3:5-8, 4:18-27

Our emotions can tell us something about what's in our hearts. But they cannot tell us whether we should *trust* what's in our hearts. We might feel angry with a friend for all kinds of reasons. Our anger might be a healthy response to their bad behaviour – or it may come from past experiences or wrong expectations. If we feel anxious, sad or hopeless a lot of the time, we may need advice from a doctor. When we step back and question strong emotions, we can start to work out where they might be coming from, and respond to them wisely.

Proverbs is one of the 'wisdom books' of the Bible. The writer knew that our hearts and emotions, like every part of us, are affected by our own sin and the sin of those around us. That's why we must take care of our hearts by avoiding the sorts of words and actions that will damage them (Proverbs 4:23-27).

Some of us may feel like our hearts are too broken to be mended. But 600 years before Jesus's birth, the prophet Jeremiah looked forward to a time when God would write the truth of his law on the hearts of those who follow him (Jeremiah 31:33-34). For Christians, that time is now. The Holy Spirit is living within us, working to change us from the inside. God understands what's in our hearts far better than we ever will. We can't always trust our feelings, but we can always trust him.

This week, question your emotions and try to work out where they are coming from.

- Can you think of a time when your emotions have led you down the wrong path?

- How do the things you say and do affect the way you feel? Are these effects good or bad?

- What are some ways you can put your trust in God more than your feelings?

*Trust in the LORD with all your heart and
lean not on your own understanding.*

Proverbs 3:5

Weekly Reflections

Good things

Hard things

Main focus

How have I questioned my emotions?

What am I grateful for?

What have I done well?

Who can I thank?

What can I do better?

Eating	😊	😐	😞
Sleep	😊	😐	😞
Exercise	😊	😐	😞

Prayer for next week

Feel #3

> *My God, my God, why have you forsaken me?*
> *Why are you so far from saving me,*
> *so far from my cries of anguish?*
>
> Psalm 22:1

Read: Psalm 22

Psalms is a book of songs written to God. Some are full of praise, thanks and wonder. Others, like this one, express doubt, pain and fear. God promises to never leave those who follow him (Deuteronomy 31:6), and in reality, he had not left David. But David still felt lost and abandoned. The best thing he could do with his feelings was to sing them to God.

In Psalm 22 we see how David questioned his emotions, and worked out how to respond to them. First, he put his trust in God by pouring out his heart to him. Then, he reminded himself of how God had helped his people in the past (v3-5). He cried out once again, then fixed his mind on the faithful care God had shown him in his own life (v6-10). As David thought about the truth of God's trustworthy love, he finally turned his pain into a prayer asking for help (v11-21). Singing his feelings to God took David on a journey that led him out of despair into fresh hope, and even praise (v22-31).

On the cross, Jesus cried out the opening words of Psalm 22 (Matthew 27:46). Jesus knew better than anyone that God had not really abandoned him. But David's words gave voice to his unbearable distress. In recalling this song, Jesus trusted his Father with his pain, and declared to those listening that his journey too would end in victory. On our own journeys, bringing our emotions to God is the first step.

> This week, bring your own emotions to God, perhaps by writing a letter, a poem or a song.

- How does it make you feel to see doubt, pain and fear expressed openly in the Bible?

- Can you think of a time when bringing painful feelings to God took you on a journey to fresh hope?

- Are there any tips you can take from David, to help you work through your own emotions?

My God, my God, why have you forsaken me?
Why are you so far from saving me,
so far from my cries of anguish?

Psalm 22:1

Weekly Reflections

Good things

Hard things

General mood

How have I brought my feelings to God?

What do I need to talk about?

How have I blessed others?

Who can I talk with?

How have others blessed me?

	:)	:|	:(
Eating			
Sleep			
Exercise			

Prayer for next week

Feel #4

> *Rejoice always, pray continually,*
> *give thanks in all circumstances;*
> *for this is God's will for you in Christ Jesus.*
>
> 1 Thessalonians 5:16-18

Read: 1 Thessalonians 5:5-24

The Bible tells us again and again to give thanks to God for the good gifts he has given us. It's so easy to take the things we have for granted. In the busyness of life it often takes real effort to notice our blessings. Paul wrote these words to the Thessalonian Christians because he knew the value of praising and thanking God. It's the right thing to do, it's good for our hearts, and it's good for our communities.

It's easy to be grateful when things are going well, and much harder when life is tough. But in some ways it's even more important when we're feeling low or anxious. When everything seems wrong, choosing to give thanks can help us remember the good things and restore our hope. The more we practise thanksgiving, the more natural it becomes, and the easier it is to recall our blessings on the harder days.

One way to get into the habit of noticing our blessings is to keep a gratitude journal, listing a few things each day. When we start to look for reasons to give thanks, even small, ordinary things will start to feel like what they really are –

precious gifts from the God who created us and our world. So whenever we feel gratitude bubble up within us, we can direct it straight to him. Psalm 136:1 is a word of celebration that's repeated several times throughout the Bible: 'Give thanks to the Lord, for he is good. His love endures forever.'

> This week, make an effort to notice your blessings and give thanks for them.

- Which blessings are you most aware of? Are there any that you forget or take for granted?

- What effect does it have on you to practise giving thanks, especially on the harder days?

- Starting with Psalm 136:1, how would you continue your own personal praise psalm?

Rejoice always, pray continually, give thanks in all circumstances; for this is God's will for you in Christ Jesus.

1 Thessalonians 5:16-18

Weekly Reflections

Good things	Hard things	Main focus

How have I practised giving thanks?

What am I proud of?

How have I spoken to myself?

Who can I celebrate with?

What has encouraged me?

Eating	☺	😐	☹
Sleep	☺	😐	☹
Exercise	☺	😐	☹

Prayer for next week

Feel Reflections

3-word summary

-
-
-

Verse to remember

What have I found challenging?

What have I found rewarding?

Favourite insight

What will I carry forward?

Feel prayer

Feel Optional Extra Bible Passages

Feel #1

- **Genesis 45:1-15**
  Joseph's emotional reunion with his brothers

- **Hosea 11:1-11**
  God expresses anger, hurt, sadness, love and compassion

Feel #3

- **Psalm 13**
  Another 'journey' psalm written by David

- **Lamentations 3**
  The writer preaches hope to him/herself in the midst of grief

Feel #2

- **Jeremiah 17:1-10, 31:31-34**
  Jeremiah identifies the problem in our hearts and prophesies God's solution

- **1 Corinthians 2**
  God's wisdom, given to us by the Holy Spirit

Feel #4

- **1 Chronicles 16:1-36**
  The Israelites thank God for keeping his promises

- **Psalm 136**
  A psalm giving thanks and praise to God

Feel Further Resources

- **Film:** *Inside Out* by Walt Disney Pictures and Pixar Animation Studios
  Not just for kids, this charming story is a great introduction to the value of all our feelings, and the danger of burying emotions we find difficult.

- **Book:** *Untangling Emotions: God's gift of emotions* by J. Alasdair Groves and Winston T. Smith
  A clear and readable look at what the Bible says about our emotions and how we can manage them well.

- **Book:** *I'm Not Supposed to Feel Like This: a Christian self-help approach to depression and anxiety* by Chris Williams, Paul Richards and Ingrid Whitton
  This practical book uses CBT to help Christians work through mental health challenges. Williams's free *Live Life to the Full* video courses are also widely recommended. Find out more at llttf.com/about-llttf.

Your Notes

Dwell

The things we think about play a big part in shaping who we become. The Bible tells us to take charge of our thoughts, and to fill our minds with things that will do us good.

Dwell #1

> *We demolish arguments and every pretension that sets itself up against the knowledge of God, and we take captive every thought to make it obedient to Christ.*
>
> 2 Corinthians 10:5

Read: 2 Corinthians 10:1-5

There are many different ways to think. From early childhood we each learn to believe certain things about ourselves and the world. As we grow up, our ways of thinking are built on basic beliefs like 'I am loved' or 'I can't do anything right'. But these beliefs may be true or false. By the time we become adults, our thinking habits may seem as automatic as breathing. We may not even be aware of the basic beliefs our automatic thoughts are built on. And they can be so familiar to us that we simply accept them as the truth. But in this letter, Paul explained how each of us can take charge of our thoughts, and line them up with God's truth.

When an automatic thought comes into our minds, we don't have to let it in right away. Instead, as Paul said, we can grab it and look at it carefully. Is this thought helpful? Does it agree with what God says? Does it build us up or tear us down?

This takes work, and may be hard at first. It can be helpful to 'capture' repetitive thoughts on paper so we can explore them later, by ourselves or with someone we trust.

Questioning our automatic thoughts can help us work out what to do with them. We can tell ourselves the truth. We can say yes to the thoughts that help us, and no to the ones that don't. Our minds are not fixed. Over time, we can teach ourselves new ways of thinking, that line up with God's truth.

> This week, look carefully at your automatic thoughts and try to bring them in line with God's truth.

- Can you identify any automatic thoughts that come into your head a lot? What basic beliefs are they built on? Do you want to say yes or no to them?

- How do your thinking habits affect how you feel and behave?

- What are some helpful ways for you to capture automatic thoughts and test them?

We demolish arguments and every pretension that sets itself up against the knowledge of God, and we take captive every thought to make it obedient to Christ.

2 Corinthians 10:5

Weekly Reflections

Good things	Hard things	General mood

How have I questioned my thoughts?

What help do I need?

What have I worried about?

Who can I ask for help?

What has calmed me down?

	🙂	😐	☹️
Eating			
Sleep			
Exercise			

Prayer for next week

Dwell #2   week beginning _____

> *The fear of the Lord – that is wisdom,*
> *and to shun evil is understanding.*
>
> Job 28:28

Read: Job 28:12-28

It's not always easy to work out what's true. Our own ways of thinking are built on basic beliefs, but it's possible that these beliefs might be false. So when we question our thoughts, we need to know what to test them against. We need to know where to find the truth. This poem in the middle of the book of Job tells us that the key to understanding ourselves, and our world, is to get to know God and follow his way of life. Psalm 86:11 calls this 'walking in truth' (KJV).

The best way to get to know God better is to spend time regularly praying and reading the Bible. Although it was written by many different people at different times, the whole Bible is inspired by God and has a lot to teach us about who he is, who we are, and how we can live well (2 Timothy 3:16). The Holy Spirit also speaks to us through the Bible, as we ask for his help. This makes it alive and personal (Hebrews 4:12).

Truth may be found in all kinds of places. God can speak through people or situations, or even directly into our minds and hearts. But to know for sure if something is true, we need to see if it agrees with his words in the Bible. When we line up our thoughts with God's truth, our lives will be built on a firm foundation (Matthew 7:24-27). And if we're ever confused about the truth, James 1:5 encourages us to ask God for wisdom. He longs to help us, and he won't let us down.

> This week, spend some time reading the Bible, and ask God to speak to you through it.

- What does wisdom mean to you? How can it help us to live well?

- Have you ever heard God speak to you? Did you test what you heard to make sure it agreed with the Bible?

- Is there a particular area where you need to know what's true? What does the Bible say about this?

The fear of the Lord – that is wisdom,
and to shun evil is understanding.

Job 28:28

Weekly Reflections

Good things	Hard things	Main focus

How has God spoken to me?

What am I grateful for?

What have I done well?

Who can I thank?

What can I do better?

Eating	☺	😐	☹
Sleep	☺	😐	☹
Exercise	☺	😐	☹

Prayer for next week

Dwell #3   week beginning _____

> *Whatever is true, whatever is noble, whatever is right,*
> *whatever is pure, whatever is lovely,*
> *whatever is admirable ... think about such things.*
>
> Philippians 4:8

Read: Philippians 4:4-9

When we look at our lives and the world around us, there's a lot that seems uncertain and out of our control. Paul knew this as well as anyone. Writing this letter from prison, he didn't know if he'd end up being set free or executed! So when Paul encouraged the Philippian Christians not to be anxious about anything, he wasn't making light of their troubles. He was sharing wise advice from his own journey: celebrate God's goodness, ask him for help, and dwell on positive things.

When we spend a lot of time thinking about something, a habit begins to form. Our minds get used to familiar topics, and keep going back to the same things. These may be thoughts that bring us joy and comfort, or ones that make us feel angry or worried. Of course, we all need to think about difficult things at times. God doesn't want us to ignore the painful parts of life. But we can choose to spend time thinking about positive things too. Whenever we fix our minds on things that bring us hope, we guide our minds towards thankfulness and praise. Dwelling on all that is 'true, pure and lovely' gives us strength to face the harder things.

Some of us may need support from a trusted friend or therapist as we practise new ways of thinking. And we all need God's help. He is near (v6), and he loves us. As verse 7 of this passage says, he longs to fill us with his perfect peace.

> This week, spend some time dwelling on positive things.

- Are there any topics you spend a lot of time thinking about? How do they make you feel?

- What are some 'true, pure and lovely' things that you would like your mind to be filled with?

- How can dwelling on positive things give you strength to face the harder things?

*Whatever is true, whatever is noble, whatever is right,
whatever is pure, whatever is lovely,
whatever is admirable ... think about such things.*

Philippians 4:8

Weekly Reflections

Good things	Hard things	General mood

What positive things have I dwelled on?

What do I need to talk about?

How have I blessed others?

Who can I talk with?

How have others blessed me?

Eating	☺	😐	☹
Sleep	☺	😐	☹
Exercise	☺	😐	☹

Prayer for next week

Dwell #4 week beginning _____

> *One thing I ask from the LORD, this only do I seek:*
> *that I may dwell in the house of the LORD all the*
> *days of my life, to gaze on the beauty of the LORD.*
>
> Psalm 27:4

Read: Psalm 27

In this famous psalm, David imagined how wonderful it would be to live in God's home with him and see him face to face every day. As Christians, we know that one day we will live forever with God. But our earthly lives are full of demands and distractions. That day when we will finally be with God can seem very far off. All the noise around us and within us can easily drown out the Holy Spirit's voice. And when that happens, God's presence with us starts to feel less real.

Like David, though, we can choose to 'gaze on the beauty of the LORD' by spending time thinking about who he is. We can remind ourselves of his faithfulness to us in the past and his promises for the future. We can praise him for his love (Psalm 103:8-18), his power (Isaiah 40:25-31), and his mercy (Titus 3:3-6). We can thank him for being with us, and think about what that means (Psalm 23). As we spend time with God in this way, the truths of his amazing goodness will be planted deep in our hearts and minds.

The Bible tells us to focus on eternal things (Colossians 3:2) and to fix our eyes on Jesus (Hebrews 12:2). As we do this, the way we think about life will change.

Through the celebrations and storms of life, our minds will dwell in a place of peace, comfort and safety, at home with God.

> This week, make time to fix your eyes on Jesus and the reality of his presence with you.

- Are there things in your life that drown out the Holy Spirit's voice and make God seem far away?

- Are there any Bible passages that help you think about who God is and what he is like?

- How might 'gazing on the beauty of the LORD' help you deal with the things you're facing at the moment?

One thing I ask from the LORD, this only do I seek: that I may dwell in the house of the LORD all the days of my life, to gaze on the beauty of the LORD.

Psalm 27:4

Weekly Reflections

Good things

Hard things

Main focus

How have I gazed on God's beauty?

What am I proud of?

How have I spoken to myself?

Who can I celebrate with?

What has encouraged me?

Eating 🙂 😐 🙁

Sleep 🙂 😐 🙁

Exercise 🙂 😐 🙁

Prayer for next week

Dwell Reflections

3-word summary

-
-
-

Verse to remember

What have I found challenging?

What have I found rewarding?

Favourite insight

What will I carry forward?

Dwell prayer

Dwell Optional Extra Bible Passages

Dwell #1

- Genesis 3

  Sin begins with believing lies instead of the truth

- Isaiah 55:8-13

  God's word is powerful and true

Dwell #3

- Matthew 6:25-34

  Jesus teaches his disciples about worrying

- 1 Peter 1:3-16

  Peter encourages Christians to focus on God's grace

Dwell #2

- Psalm 119:1-48

  A psalm praising the truth and goodness of God's law

- 2 Timothy 3:1 – 4:5

  Studying the Bible helps us to know the truth

Dwell #4

- Psalm 84

  Another psalm about dwelling in God's presence

- Isaiah 40

  Gazing on God's power, love, glory and grace

Dwell Further Resources

- **Book:** *How to Read the Bible for All Its Worth* by Gordon D. Fee and Douglas Stuart

  This excellent guide introduces each type of writing we find in the Bible, including poetry, narrative, prophecy and more. It's really helpful for working out how to read and understand different parts of the Bible.

- **Book:** *The Grumbler's Guide to Giving Thanks: reclaiming the gifts of a lost spiritual discipline* by Dustin Crowe

  A brilliant in-depth study of thanksgiving as worship and a God-given path to joy. Clear and inspiring, with tips on how to make this a habit.

- **Art Book:** *More Than Words* by Hannah Dunnett

  Dunnett incorporates dozens of Bible verses into each of her unique paintings, with themes including God's goodness and his delight in us. A wonderful focus for Bible study, reflection or simple enjoyment.

Your Notes

Receive

Grace is a gift that none of us could ever deserve. If we want to truly understand God's amazing grace towards us, it's not enough to just read about it. We need to bathe in it, letting it soak into every corner of our hearts.

Receive #1 week beginning _____

> *I have the desire to do what is good, but I cannot carry it out. For I do not do the good I want to do, but the evil I do not want to do – this I keep on doing.*
>
> Romans 7:18-19

Read: Romans 7:7-25

Before Paul became a follower of Jesus, he was a teacher of the Jewish law. Like many around him, Paul worked hard to obey every part of this God-given pattern for life. But he found that even though the law told him what was right, it couldn't help him *do* what was right. Instead of proving his goodness, the law showed up everything wrong in his heart.

The Bible says that human beings are 'slaves to sin' (John 8:34). However much we want to do what's right, we find we can't even live up to our own standards all the time – never mind God's! Sin has a hold on us, and we are too weak to escape its clutches. We are guilty of disobeying God, but we are also helpless prisoners, unable to free ourselves. No wonder Paul saw himself as 'wretched' (v24)!

But where the law brought guilt and shame, Jesus brings good news: freedom and forgiveness. Through his death, Jesus took the punishment for our sin. He paid the price to release us from our slavery. We are now free to turn away from the destructive sin that once separated us from God (Isaiah 59:2).

We can choose instead to trust in Jesus and live life God's way. This is what the Bible calls 'repentance'. We will still fail at times, but sin has lost its hold on us. Like Paul, we know we can't obey the whole law. But we are rescued by our hope in the only one who could, and did: Jesus himself.

> This week, reflect on Jesus as the one who rescues you from slavery to sin.

- Have you ever felt that sin had a hold on you? How did this affect you?

- What does repentance mean to you? Does it go beyond saying sorry?

- In what ways has trusting Jesus brought freedom into your life?

I have the desire to do what is good, but I cannot carry it out. For I do not do the good I want to do, but the evil I do not want to do – this I keep on doing.

Romans 7:18-19

Weekly Reflections

Good things	Hard things	General mood

How have I turned away from sin?

What help do I need?

What have I worried about?

Who can I ask for help?

What has calmed me down?

Eating	☺	😐	☹
Sleep	☺	😐	☹
Exercise	☺	😐	☹

Prayer for next week

Receive #2 week beginning _____

> *It is by grace you have been saved, through faith –*
> *and this is not from yourselves, it is the gift of God –*
> *not by any works, so that no one can boast.*
>
> **Ephesians 2:8-9**

Read: Ephesians 1:15 – 2:10

The heart of the good news is that God saved us when we could not save ourselves. Paul's letters are full of this truth. He had to keep reminding the churches in his care that their own efforts had got them nowhere. It was only God's 'rich mercy' that had secured their place in his family (Ephesians 2:4-5). Grace is an undeserved gift – it cannot be earned!

Paul knew this truth would be easy to forget. When we feel we're doing well, we can be tempted to rely on our own ability, and take pride in how 'good' we are. When we feel we've messed up, our failures can lead us to shame, or even despair. The truth is that when it comes to salvation, neither our sins nor our virtues count for anything. There is no heavenly scale tilting one way and then the other, as it weighs our good deeds against the wrong we do. If there was, even our best efforts could never cancel out the wrongs we have done (Isaiah 64:6). But on the scale of God's grace, there is only the weight of Jesus's goodness. He tips the balance forever in our favour, as long as we continue to trust in him.

The power of God to save us is the same power that raised Jesus from death (Ephesians 1:19-20). Nothing we do can beat that! Even the faith to believe is a gift from God (Romans 12:3). All we have to do is choose daily to keep trusting and following Jesus as best we can. He will handle the rest.

> This week, remind yourself that your place in God's family is a free gift of grace, not earned by your own efforts.

- Can you think of a time when you relied on your own goodness or despaired of your sinfulness?

- What might a scale of your good and bad actions look like? How does it feel to think that none of those things count towards your salvation, or against it?

- What truth about God's grace do you need to keep in mind? How can you do this?

It is by grace you have been saved, through faith –
and this is not from yourselves, it is the gift of God –
not by any works, so that no one can boast.

Ephesians 2:8-9

Weekly Reflections

Good things

Hard things

Main focus

When have I appreciated God's grace?

What am I grateful for?

What have I done well?

Who can I thank?

What can I do better?

Eating	🙂	😐	🙁
Sleep	🙂	😐	🙁
Exercise	🙂	😐	🙁

Prayer for next week

Receive #3 week beginning _____

> *It is for freedom that Christ has set us free.*
> *Stand firm, then, and do not let yourselves*
> *be burdened again by a yoke of slavery.*
>
> Galatians 5:1

Read: Galatians 5:1-14

'You foolish Galatians!' Paul exclaimed in Galatians 3:1. 'Who has bewitched you?' This letter is full of emotion – by the strength of Paul's words, we might think there was some terrible sin causing scandal in the Galatian church. In fact, the problem was much more serious than that.

To join the Jewish community, a man had to be circumcised and agree to obey the Old Testament law. Some teachers were now telling the Galatian Christians that they must do this too. Paul wrote to beg the Galatians to say no. The law was given to show people that they *couldn't* obey it. They were slaves to sin and desperately needed to be rescued. And now God's promised Saviour had come! Jesus paid for our freedom with his own blood (1 Peter 1:18-19). So if we add conditions to salvation and rely on our own efforts to earn it, we put ourselves right back under the burden of the law. We lose the victory Jesus won for us. We lose grace.

But the gift of God's grace does not give us permission to sin. Jesus has beaten sin! He saved us from its clutches and took away its power, so that we would be free to follow God without fear (Luke 1:74). Through grace, we have peace and friendship with our creator, a new start and a new purpose. Sin has nothing to offer us – everything good is found in Jesus. As John 5:24 says, we have passed from death into life.

This week, think about any ways you've been tempted to add something extra to grace.

- Do you find it surprising that Paul was so upset by this issue in the Galatian church?

- What problems can it cause if we rely on our own efforts to earn salvation?

- Are there any particular sins that still tempt you? What do they claim to offer you? How can you resist them?

It is for freedom that Christ has set us free.
Stand firm, then, and do not let yourselves
be burdened again by a yoke of slavery.

Galatians 5:1

Weekly Reflections

Good things

Hard things

General mood

How have I experienced God's freedom?

What do I need to talk about?

How have I blessed others?

Who can I talk with?

How have others blessed me?

Eating   😊 😐 🙁

Sleep   😊 😐 🙁

Exercise   😊 😐 🙁

Prayer for next week

Receive #4   week beginning _____

> *Should I not have concern for the great city of Nineveh, in which there are more than a hundred and twenty thousand people who cannot tell their right hand from their left...?*
>
> Jonah 4:11

Read: Jonah 3:3 – 4:11

God saw that Nineveh was full of sin. He called his prophet Jonah to warn the city that they would soon be punished. But Jonah ran away! He knew that God was loving and merciful (Jonah 4:2). He didn't want to give the Ninevites a chance to turn from their evil lives and receive forgiveness. But in the end this is exactly what happened, and Jonah was furious.

The scandal of God's grace is that it's given to people who don't deserve it. He longs to show mercy even to those who treat us badly, abuse their power or attack our country. This may seem very wrong to us, as it did to Jonah. Even though we ourselves are grateful for God's free gift of grace, it can be hard to desire mercy and forgiveness for people who have hurt us.

God's grace is for everyone. That makes some people angry, and others relieved. If we hold onto the idea that we can please God through our efforts, it's an outrage to see 'bad' people getting the blessings we've worked so hard for (Luke 15:28-30).

But God asks us to look at things differently. Jesus had compassion on the crowds because they were 'harassed and helpless, like sheep without a shepherd' (Matthew 9:36). When we see those around us through God's eyes, we will share his love for the lost, confused people of this world. And like him, we will long to see them receive mercy and grace.

> This week, think about God's longing to show grace towards people you find hard to love.

- How do you feel about the story of Jonah? Why do you think it's in the Bible?

- What people or groups do you think of as 'enemies' in your life and in the wider world?

- Is it easy for you to share God's desire for those people to be forgiven and blessed?

Should I not have concern for the great city of Nineveh, in which there are more than a hundred and twenty thousand people who cannot tell their right hand from their left...?

Jonah 4:11

Weekly Reflections

Good things

Hard things

Main focus

How have I shown grace to others?

What am I proud of?

How have I spoken to myself?

Who can I celebrate with?

What has encouraged me?

Eating	🙂	😐	☹️
Sleep	🙂	😐	☹️
Exercise	🙂	😐	☹️

Prayer for next week

Receive Reflections

3-word summary

-
-
-

Verse to remember

What have I found challenging?

What have I found rewarding?

Favourite insight

What will I carry forward?

Receive prayer

Receive Optional Extra Bible Passages

Receive #1

- Psalm 51
  David prays for forgiveness

- Romans 3:9-24
  No one is good, but all can be saved through Jesus

Receive #3

- Galatians 3
  Paul explains why grace is better than law

- 1 John 4:7 – 5:5
  Living a life of love by the Spirit

Receive #2

- 2 Chronicles 20:1-30
  God fights on behalf of his people

- Romans 4
  Faith in God is counted as righteousness

Receive #4

- Luke 15
  Parables showing God's mercy towards those who are lost

- Acts 2:14-41
  Peter's sermon at Pentecost, offering grace to everyone

Receive Further Resources

- **Book:** *The Truth About Us: the very good news about how very bad we are* by Brant Hansen

  A down-to-earth, generous and funny look at our deep need for grace, and how Jesus changes everything. There's a great two-part interview with Hansen about the book at branthansen.com/?s=hammock+street.

- **Video Talk**: *Grace Upon Grace* by Matt Chandler

  A more intellectual, in-depth look at grace, what it means for us and how God's law fits into the picture. Available to watch on YouTube and at tvcresources.net/resource-library/sermons/grace-upon-grace/.

- **Book**: *What's So Amazing About Grace?* by Philip Yancey

  In this easy-to-read book, Yancey explores what grace looks like in action, and how we can allow grace to shape our lives as followers of Jesus.

Your Notes

Become

The world is full of voices telling us who we are, and who we should be. The Bible tells us to listen instead to God's voice, and find our identity in what he says about us.

Become #1   week beginning _____

> *He chose us in him before the creation of the*
> *world . . . In love he predestined us for adoption*
> *to sonship through Jesus Christ, in accordance*
> *with his pleasure and will.*
>
> Ephesians 1:4-5

Read: Ephesians 1:3-14

When we reflect on who we are, we might think about our personality traits, achievements, cultural heritage or important relationships. These things may be significant parts of us, but Paul viewed them all as secondary. In this passage, he gave us a wonderful and eternal answer to the question of who we are. Each one of us is a beloved child of God, chosen by him before he even created the world.

Whatever roles we might take on and whatever groups we belong to, our first and most important identity is this one. God looks on us with the affection of a devoted father. It makes him happy to spend time with us! At any time of the day or night he is always ready to welcome, comfort, guide and bless his precious sons and daughters. Nothing in our lives can change the reality of God's love for us (Romans 8:38-39).

Many things in our lives have real value. But none of those things determine *our* value. If we attach our worth and identity to them, we will end up disappointed. Instead, we must make

God's love for us the centre of who we are, and attach our worth and identity to him alone. In his love, we are set free. Free from comparing ourselves to others. Free from finding our value in things that cannot satisfy us. Free at last to become the unique people God created each of us to be.

> This week, think about your identity as God's precious child, chosen and loved by him.

- What comes to mind when you reflect on who you are? Has this changed through your life?

- Have you ever attached your identity to something and ended up disappointed?

- What does it mean to you to make God's love for you the centre of who you are? How might this be freeing?

He chose us in him before the creation of the world ...
In love he predestined us for adoption to sonship through
Jesus Christ, in accordance with his pleasure and will.

Ephesians 1:4-5

Weekly Reflections

Good things

Hard things

General mood

How have I found my identity in God's love for me?

What help do I need?

What have I worried about?

Who can I ask for help?

What has calmed me down?

Eating   🙂   😐   ☹️

Sleep   🙂   😐   ☹️

Exercise   🙂   😐   ☹️

Prayer for next week

Become #2 week beginning _____

> *If anyone is in Christ, the new creation has come:*
> *the old has gone, the new is here!*
>
> 2 Corinthians 5:17

Read: 2 Corinthians 5:11 – 6:2

Many people think the Bible is just a book of rules to follow. The wonderful truth is that we are saved not by being good, but simply by trusting Jesus. But this isn't the full story. As Paul wrote to the Corinthian church, when someone trusts Jesus, they become a 'new creation'. The Holy Spirit comes to live within them and changes them from the inside out. We were loved and accepted 'while we were still sinners' (Romans 5:8). Now, though, we have God's constant help and strength to follow the life-giving path of obedience to him.

That doesn't mean we won't ever get things wrong. But we have God's strength on our side. The Holy Spirit's power works in us, with us and through us. He leads us into victories we couldn't win by ourselves. Giving our lives to Jesus is the opposite of self-help. It's accepting *God's* help, inviting him to remake our hearts and our lives for his glory, and for our good (Psalm 51:10).

Knowing that we are new creations should give us the confidence to keep saying no to our old ways of life. Asking God for his help and strength gives us the power to choose the right paths. And trusting in Jesus keeps us from despair when we fail. Our loving creator is recreating us. He is moulding us into the people he always meant us to be. This truly is something beautifully, wonderfully new.

> This week, spend some time with God, asking for help and strength to obey him.

- How easy is it to believe that you are a new creation in Jesus? How does it make you feel?

- What evidence of change can you see in your life since you've been a Christian?

- Can you think of a time when you have experienced the Holy Spirit's power helping you to do what's right?

If anyone is in Christ, the new creation has come:
the old has gone, the new is here!

2 Corinthians 5:17

Weekly Reflections

Good things

Hard things

Main focus

How has the Holy Spirit helped me do what's right?

What am I grateful for?

What have I done well?

Who can I thank?

What can I do better?

Eating	☺	😐	☹
Sleep	☺	😐	☹
Exercise	☺	😐	☹

Prayer for next week

Become #3   week beginning _____

> *You will receive power when the Holy Spirit*
> *comes on you; and you will be my witnesses...*
> *to the ends of the earth.*
>
> Acts 1:8

Read: Acts 1:1-11

Before Jesus returned to heaven, he left his disciples with a job to do. He told them to spread the word about his death and resurrection, and 'make disciples of all nations' (Matthew 28:18-20). But these men had run away in fear when Jesus was arrested! They weren't brave enough for the task ahead. Everything changed a week later, when the disciples were filled with the Holy Spirit (Acts 2). These weak and frightened men became bold! They spent the rest of their lives declaring the good news about Jesus to anyone who would listen.

The disciples were eyewitnesses to Jesus's death and resurrection. We weren't there to see these things, but we believe the testimonies of those who wrote about them in the Bible. And we have seen God's work in our own lives, and in the lives of the people we know. Just like the disciples, we are Jesus's representatives on earth. We too are filled with the Holy Spirit. We can point people to Jesus by living in a way that pleases God, and by sharing our faith with others.

The thought of telling people about Jesus can seem scary or awkward, but it doesn't need to be that way. In fact, God wants it to flow naturally out of who we are, by the power of the Holy Spirit within us. The first step is to prepare an answer for anyone who asks about 'the hope that you have' (1 Peter 3:15). Then we can ask God to give us opportunities to try it out!

This week, ask God to give you opportunities to talk about your faith with others.

- In what ways does your life point to Jesus?

- How do you feel about telling people about your faith? How might it flow naturally out of who you are?

- How would you answer someone who asked about 'the hope that you have'?

*You will receive power when the Holy Spirit comes on you;
and you will be my witnesses ... to the ends of the earth.*

Acts 1:8

Weekly Reflections

Good things

Hard things

General mood

How have I pointed people to Jesus?

What do I need to talk about?

How have I blessed others?

Who can I talk with?

How have others blessed me?

Eating	☺	😐	☹
Sleep	☺	😐	☹
Exercise	☺	😐	☹

Prayer for next week

Become #4 week beginning _____

> *In all my prayers for all of you, I always pray with joy... being confident... that he who began a good work in you will carry it on to completion until the day of Christ Jesus.*
>
> Philippians 1:4, 6

Read: Philippians 1:1-11

When we've been following Jesus for a while, we start to realise that it hasn't made us perfect. We may still struggle with some of the same old sins. We still hurt other people and make mistakes. It can be disappointing to realise that change is happening much slower than we'd like.

God does sometimes give us miraculous breakthroughs in particular areas. But overall, we become more like Jesus gradually. Sometimes it may feel like we're taking two steps forward and one step back. Further on in the journey we may see more clearly how far we've come, but also how far we have still to go. But working together with the Holy Spirit who lives within us, change does come. It gets easier day by day to make good choices, to love well, and to worship God joyfully.

Paul knew that following Jesus didn't mean instant transformation. But he also knew that we are in safe hands. God has promised to keep changing us (2 Corinthians 3:18), and to never leave us or give up on us (Hebrews 13:5). We can trust that he will finish what he started. If we ever feel frustrated by the wrong we still do, our guilt should lead us not to turn away from our Saviour, but to turn back to him. The God who forgives us and heals us has flung our sins far away from us (Psalm 103:12) – he declares us innocent! And he will keep working in us until he completes the job.

> This week, look back on your journey with Jesus so far, and think about the work God is doing in you.

- What does it look like to work together with the Holy Spirit? What is your responsibility, and what is his?

- How do you feel about the sin that's still in your life? Are these feelings helpful? Where do they lead you?

- How might knowing you are secure in God's hands help you deal more effectively with your sin?

*In all my prayers for all of you, I always pray
with joy ... being confident ... that he who began
a good work in you will carry it on to completion
until the day of Christ Jesus.*

Philippians 1:4, 6

Weekly Reflections

Good things

Hard things

Main focus

How have I worked together with the Holy Spirit?

What am I proud of?

How have I spoken to myself?

Who can I celebrate with?

What has encouraged me?

Eating ☺ ☺ ☹

Sleep ☺ ☺ ☹

Exercise ☺ ☺ ☹

Prayer for next week

Become Reflections

3-word summary

-
-
-

Verse to remember

What have I found challenging?

What have I found rewarding?

Favourite insight

What will I carry forward?

Become prayer

Become Optional Extra Bible Passages

Become #1

- 1 John 3
  Living as beloved children of God

- Hebrews 2:5-18
  Jesus is our loving brother

Become #3

- Matthew 5:1-16
  Encouragement to be open about our faith

- 1 Peter 3:1-16
  Jesus can be seen in us by our words and actions

Become #2

- Joel 2:18-32
  Joel prophesies God pouring out his Spirit on all his people

- Romans 5:1-9, 6:1-14
  Our old selves have died with Jesus

Become #4

- John 10:1-30
  Jesus is the Good Shepherd who keeps his sheep safe

- Romans 8:1-13
  Even when we sin we are not condemned

Become Further Resources

- **Book:** *The Purpose Driven Life: what on earth am I here for?* by Rick Warren

  A step by step look at what God says about who we are and the meaning of our lives. A great overview, especially for new Christians.

- **Art book:** *Beholding and Becoming: the art of everyday worship* by Ruth Chou Simons

  A beautiful collection of reflections on growing into our identity as God's children. Simons' lovely nature-inspired paintings bring life to her words.

- **Video Talk:** *Trueface Two Roads FULL Message* by John Lynch

  In an entertaining 45 minutes, Lynch powerfully shows us how God's grace and love give followers of Jesus a whole new identity. Lynch is a brilliant storyteller, and this talk is based on his book *The Cure*. Watch online on YouTube and at trueface.org/videos.

Your Notes

Know

The key to living a healthy Christian life is to spend time with God as often as we can. It's here that we get to know him and learn to recognise his voice.

Know #1

> *Show me your ways, LORD, teach me your paths.*
> *Guide me in your truth and teach me, for you are*
> *God my Saviour, and my hope is in you all day long.*
>
> *Psalm 25:4-5*

Read: Psalm 25

God wants more than just our obedience. He created us for relationship with him. He wants us to enjoy spending time in his presence. In this psalm, King David spoke of his longing to know God better and learn more about him. Other parts of the Bible encourage us to draw near to God (James 4:8) and come before his throne (Hebrews 4:16). Our God is not a distant judge up in the clouds. He is close and caring, eager to hear and help us. He is our Father, our friend and our King.

We can talk to God anywhere and at any time. He wants to be involved in every part of our lives. But if we really want to get to know him, it helps to set aside regular times when we can meet with him and not be distracted. A busy husband and wife may plan date nights when they can really focus on each other, rather than cooking dinner or bathing the baby. It's the same with God. It's important to spend quality time alone with him if we want our relationship to grow.

In our meetings with God, we can read the Bible and talk to him, or be quiet and give him space to speak to us. We may choose to follow daily readings and prayers, or leave the time open and free. We can pour our hearts out to God in the lounge or on a long walk. However we choose to do it, these meetings are precious and powerful. God will use our time with him to shape us into the people he created us to be.

This week, think about how your relationship with God has grown through time alone with him.

- What are some things that help you get into the habit of meeting regularly with God?

- What is your experience of spending time with God like? Do you enjoy it? Is your relationship with him growing?

- What are some of the different ways you can spend time with God? Which of these appeal to you most?

Show me your ways, LORD, teach me your paths.
Guide me in your truth and teach me, for you are
God my Saviour, and my hope is in you all day long.

Psalm 25:4-5

Weekly Reflections

Good things	Hard things	General mood

How have I spent quality time with God?

What help do I need?

What have I worried about?

Who can I ask for help?

What has calmed me down?

Eating	🙂	😐	🙁
Sleep	🙂	😐	🙁
Exercise	🙂	😐	🙁

Prayer for next week

Know #2   week beginning _____

> *How sweet are your words to my taste,*
> *sweeter than honey to my mouth!*
>
> Psalm 119:103

Read: Psalm 119:89-112

In Psalm 119, the longest chapter in the Bible, the writer sings joyfully about how much he loves God's written teachings. Such excitement about the Bible might seem strange at first. Not all of us enjoy reading, and most of us find some parts of the Bible confusing or unsettling. But when we invite the Holy Spirit to help us, he breathes life into the words. When we take time to read slowly and let it all sink in, the Bible becomes nourishing food for our souls.

There are as many different ways to read the Bible as there are ways to enjoy a feast. We can explore one single verse and look at it from different angles, noticing the 'flavour' of each word. Or we can read several chapters to get a sense of how all the ingredients fit together. What does the passage tell us about God, and about us? How does it relate to our lives? If we have more time, we might study a section more closely. We can imagine ourselves in the scene, rewrite it in our own words, or paint it as a picture. Different Bible translations, audio Bibles and commentaries can all be helpful tools to understand God's teachings better.

In our journeys through the Bible, our guide is the God who inspired these words. He longs to share his thoughts with us. And there really is sweetness in his teachings. As Psalm 34:8 says, we will 'taste and see that the LORD is good'.

> This week, try some different ways of reading this week's passage.

- How do you feel about the Bible? Which parts do you enjoy? Which parts do you find hard?

- What Bible study methods and tools could you use to help you understand the Bible better?

- Where have you tasted the sweetness in God's teachings?

How sweet are your words to my taste,
sweeter than honey to my mouth!

Psalm 119:103

Weekly Reflections

Good things

Hard things

Main focus

What have I learned from the Bible?

What am I grateful for?

What have I done well?

Who can I thank?

What can I do better?

Eating	🙂	😐	☹️
Sleep	🙂	😐	☹️
Exercise	🙂	😐	☹️

Prayer for next week

Know #3

> *Our Father in heaven, hallowed be your name,*
> *your kingdom come, your will be done,*
> *on earth as it is in heaven.*
>
> Matthew 6:9-10

Read: Matthew 6:5-13

These are some of the most famous words in the whole Bible. When we pray the Lord's Prayer, we're joining in with millions of Christians throughout history. People still pray it every day in homes, churches, schools and hospitals across the whole world. So it's a great place to start if we're not sure how to pray. We can even adapt each line to talk about our own personal sins and needs, and to thank him for our blessings.

Some people think prayer is just a way to ask God for things we want. But the Lord's Prayer, taught by Jesus himself, shows us that it's much more than that. It's not only telling God what's on our hearts; it's also asking him what's on his heart. It helps us to focus on him. It lines us up with his vision for the world, and for our own lives. But this prayer isn't a magic formula. We don't need special words to get God's attention! We can talk to him any time, anywhere, about anything at all.

As with any conversation, prayer also involves listening. When we sit quietly with God, we may find he speaks to us through a Bible verse, or into our thoughts. It can be hard to tell if a thought is from God, so it's important to test whether it agrees with what he says in the Bible, and talk to a wise friend if we're unsure. As we get to know God more deeply, we will start to recognise his voice (John 10:27). It's through prayer that he works to untangle our minds and soften our hearts.

This week, spend some time talking and listening to God.

- How easy do you find it to pray?

- In your prayer times, do you spend more time talking or listening? In what ways do you think God speaks to you?

- How has your friendship with God grown through prayer?

Our Father in heaven, hallowed be your name,
your kingdom come, your will be done,
on earth as it is in heaven.

Matthew 6:9-10

Weekly Reflections

Good things

Hard things

General mood

How have I connected with God through prayer?

What do I need to talk about?

How have I blessed others?

Who can I talk with?

How have others blessed me?

Eating	🙂	😐	🙁
Sleep	🙂	😐	🙁
Exercise	🙂	😐	🙁

Prayer for next week

Know #4

> *Let us... spur one another on towards love and*
> *good deeds, not giving up meeting together...*
> *but encouraging one another.*
>
> Hebrews 10:24-25

Read: Hebrews 10:19-25

Faith is a long and sometimes difficult journey. We are not meant to travel alone. Time on our own with God is a big part of the Christian life, but we also need to get to know him in community. Praying, worshipping and learning with other followers of Jesus helps to keep our faith going. Together, we grow in friendship with God, and grow together as his family. When the journey gets tough, our fellow Christians can pray for us, encourage us and help us to stay on the right path.

Seeing a good friend with their new husband or wife for the first time can be surprising. Seeing how our friend acts with someone else and getting a glimpse of this other relationship might show us parts of their personality that we haven't seen before. It can deepen our understanding of who they are. Worshipping God alongside other Christians is a little like that. Because each of us is different, our relationships with God are different too.

God is greater than we can imagine. In many ways he is a mystery to us, and no one person can understand him fully. But as we get to know him, we each grasp different pieces of the puzzle of who he is. That's why it helps to talk to other Christians and share what we're each learning about God. When we fit our puzzle pieces together, we all gain a bigger picture of the God we worship.

This week, talk to a Christian friend and share what you're each learning about God.

- How does your friendship with God reflect your personality?

- What have you learned recently about God? Can you use this to encourage another Christian?

- Can you think of a time when someone else has helped you see something new about God?

Let us ... spur one another on towards love and good deeds, not giving up meeting together ... but encouraging one another.

Hebrews 10:24-25

Weekly Reflections

Good things	Hard things	Main focus

Who am I travelling with on my faith journey?

What am I proud of?

How have I spoken to myself?

Who can I celebrate with?

What has encouraged me?

	🙂	😐	☹️
Eating			
Sleep			
Exercise			

Prayer for next week

Know Reflections

3-word summary

-
-
-

Verse to remember

What have I found challenging?

What have I found rewarding?

Favourite insight

What will I carry forward?

Know prayer

Know Optional Extra Bible Passages

Know #1

- Luke 5:16, Mark 1:35-37
  Jesus practised regular quiet times with God

- John 15:1-17
  Encouragement to stay connected to Jesus

Know #3

- Luke 10:38-42
  Mary is praised for choosing to listen to Jesus

- 1 Timothy 2:1-7
  Praying for governments and for people to know Jesus

Know #2

- Joshua 1:1-9
  God commands Joshua to study and follow his written law

- 2 Kings 22:1 – 23:25
  King Josiah finds God's law and obeys it

Know #4

- Luke 2:41-52
  As a boy, Jesus learns from others and shares his insights

- Acts 2:42-46
  The early Christians meet and pray together

Know Further Resources

- **Book:** *How to Pray* by Pete Greig
  A simple and helpful guide to all the different ways we can pray, using the Lord's Prayer as a starting point.

- **TV Series:** *The Chosen* by Dallas Jenkins
  An excellent and thought-provoking new drama series about the life of Jesus and his disciples. Watch for free on their YouTube channel, or by downloading *The Chosen* app on any Apple or Android device.

- **Videos and Manual:** *The Bible Course* by the Bible Society
  An excellent teaching course that gives an overview of the whole Bible and how it all fits together. Available to buy online at biblesociety.org.uk/explore-the-bible/the-bible-course/

Your Notes

Follow

Faith is much more than just believing in God. It's also putting our trust in his loving kindness and choosing to make him our King. True faith is following God's lead in our journey through life.

Follow #1

> *He has shown you, O mortal, what is good. And what does the LORD require of you? To act justly and to love mercy and to walk humbly with your God.*
>
> **Micah 6:8**

Read: Micah 6:1-8

Most of us want to control our own lives, make our own choices and go our own way. But the Bible tells us that we don't belong to ourselves. We were created by God, and we belong to him (Psalm 100:3). The first human sin was pride: when Adam and Eve disobeyed God, they were rejecting his authority over their lives (Genesis 3:1-6). So a life of faith in God has to begin with humility. We start by bowing down before him, and promising to follow him as our King. This has to happen in our hearts. We can't pretend with God. Church services, prayer meetings and public sacrifices are worth nothing, if our hearts are far from his (Amos 5:21-24). Truly worshipping him is not about putting on a show – it's about taking him seriously and caring about the things he cares about. The prophet Micah's message reveals what's in God's heart. He wants his people to do what's right, treat each other fairly, and embrace kindness and forgiveness.

It's wonderful to follow a king like this. Here is a God who defends the innocent and dies on behalf of the guilty. He uses his power to protect the weak, and invites the poor to share his riches. He is always good, always loving and always faithful.

Proverbs 3:6 assures us that when we choose to follow God instead of our own desires, he will always lead us in the right direction. Our King is a king we can trust.

> This week, think about what it means to walk humbly with God.

- How easy is it for you to accept God as your King? Do you think of yourself as belonging to him?

- What does it look like to act justly, love mercy and walk humbly with God in your life?

- What are some things that God has shown you he cares about? How have you responded?

He has shown you, O mortal, what is good. And what does the L<small>ORD</small> require of you? To act justly and to love mercy and to walk humbly with your God.

Micah 6:8

Weekly Reflections

Good things

Hard things

General mood

How have I taken God seriously?

What help do I need?

What have I worried about?

Who can I ask for help?

What has calmed me down?

Eating	☺	😐	☹
Sleep	☺	😐	☹
Exercise	☺	😐	☹

Prayer for next week

Follow #2 week beginning _____

> *Show me your faith without deeds,*
> *and I will show you my faith by my deeds.*
>
> James 2:18

Read: James 1:22-25, 2:14-24

Some people think being a Christian is just about what we believe. But this passage tells us there are two parts to following Jesus. First, we must put our trust in him as our Saviour. This is what the Bible calls 'faith'. And second, we must try to do what he says is right. The Bible calls this 'faithfulness'. With God, faith and faithfulness go together. We can't have one without the other.

James knew that we are all saved by God's grace – a free gift that none of us can earn. But he was certain that real faith would show itself in a person's behaviour. Experiencing God's amazing grace should change us! When we receive his love, we will want to love him in return (1 John 4:19). When we see how our sin hurts him, we won't carry on as if it doesn't matter (1:23-24). When we truly see how gentle and kind our Father is, we will want to live the way he says is best.

Faithfulness is faith put into action. We live faithfully by believing God's truth, and making sure it affects how we think and act. We invite him to guide us through the ups and downs of life. And we keep putting our trust in him, even when things don't seem to make sense. This kind of active faith is powerful and life changing. We are made to faithfully follow our perfectly faithful God.

This week, think about how you are living faithfully in your daily life.

- How are faith and faithfulness related? Can you have one without the other?

- Can you think of any ways that your faith in God has affected how you think and act?

- When do you find it hardest to live faithfully?

Show me your faith without deeds,
and I will show you my faith by my deeds.

James 2:18

Weekly Reflections

Good things

Hard things

Main focus

How have I lived faithfully?

What am I grateful for?

What have I done well?

Who can I thank?

What can I do better?

Eating	☺	😐	☹
Sleep	☺	😐	☹
Exercise	☺	😐	☹

Prayer for next week

Follow #3

> *Since we live by the Spirit,*
> *let us keep in step with the Spirit.*
>
> Galatians 5:25

Read: Galatians 5:16-25

As we walk faithfully with God, our lives will start to change. With the help of the Holy Spirit who lives within us, we make small choices each day to do what's right. Over time, as he heals and strengthens our hearts, these choices become easier and more natural. Without the Holy Spirit, our attempts at self-improvement can be frustrating and limited. But when God's power is at work in our lives, everything changes. He honours our obedience and takes us further than we can ever dream of going by ourselves (Ephesians 3:20).

In this passage, Paul gave us a colourful picture of the healthy Christian life. If we see apples growing on a tree, we know that it's an apple tree! And when people see love, joy and peace growing in our lives, it's a clear sign that we belong to Jesus.

The Holy Spirit also gives us spiritual gifts, which glorify God and help us to do his will (1 Corinthians 12:7-11).

The more closely we follow Jesus, the more we will see the Holy Spirit's work in our lives. Paul called this 'keeping in step with the Spirit'. The Christian life is about walking with God and asking him to lead us each day. This is the way into the wonderful life Jesus promised (John 10:10). God has personal plans for each one of us. As we let the fruit of the Spirit grow in our lives and use the spiritual gifts he gives us, our new life with him will begin to take shape.

This week, ask God to guide you through each day.

- Which of the fruits of the Spirit do you see growing in yourself?

- What does it mean to 'keep in step with the Spirit'? How can you do this in your own life?

- Are there any areas of your life where you would especially like God's personal guidance?

Since we live by the Spirit,
let us keep in step with the Spirit.

Galatians 5:25

Weekly Reflections

Good things	Hard things	General mood

How has God guided me?

What do I need to talk about?

How have I blessed others?

Who can I talk with?

How have others blessed me?

Eating			
Sleep			
Exercise			

Prayer for next week

Follow #4

> *'I am the Lord's servant,'* Mary answered.
> *'May your word to me be fulfilled.'*
>
> Luke 1:38

Read: Luke 1:26-38

One of the hard things about life is that we can't see into the future. None of us knows even what will happen tomorrow. Dealing with this uncertainty can be hard. Some of us put our faith in careful planning. Others are tempted by fortune-telling and other spiritual practices that God forbids (Deuteronomy 18:10-11). Many of us simply try not to think too hard about what the future might hold. For Christians, following God doesn't take away the uncertainty of life. But trusting his goodness and fatherly love can give us confidence as we step into the unknown.

Mary was probably only a teenager when an angel told her she would give birth to God's promised Saviour. She had no idea of the joys, challenges and heartbreak that lay ahead of her in this journey. But she knew that God was good. Even though this wasn't her plan and she didn't fully understand it, Mary said yes to God's vision for her life. She was certain of his faithful love, and she trusted him through all that followed.

The pieces of our own lives are shifting all the time. With all we have going on, it can be easy to get distracted and drift away from God. It takes effort to trust him through the twists and turns of life and to steadily keep following his lead. Hebrews 6:19 imagines our faith in Jesus as an anchor, holding us safely and firmly, as long as we cling to him.

This week, think about how to keep trusting God in the uncertainty of life.

- How do you feel about the uncertainty of the future? Have you ever tried to predict or control it?

- How do you think you might respond if God's vision for your life turns out to be different from your own?

- What are some practical ways to keep trusting and following Jesus through the twists and turns of life?

'I am the Lord's servant,' Mary answered.
'May your word to me be fulfilled.'

Luke 1:38

Weekly Reflections

Good things

Hard things

Main focus

How have I trusted God?

What am I proud of?

How have I spoken to myself?

Who can I celebrate with?

What has encouraged me?

Eating	☺	😐	☹
Sleep	☺	😐	☹
Exercise	☺	😐	☹

Prayer for next week

Follow Reflections

3-word summary

-
-
-

Verse to remember

What have I found challenging?

What have I found rewarding?

Favourite insight

What will I carry forward?

Follow prayer

Follow Optional Extra Bible Passages

Follow #1

- Amos 5
  Another message about the true worship God wants

- Psalm 103
  A psalm about God's character and goodness

Follow #3

- 1 Corinthians 2
  The Holy Spirit reveals God's thoughts to us

- 1 Corinthians 12:1-11, 28-31
  Spiritual gifts given to each of us by the Holy Spirit

Follow #2

- Hebrews 11
  A look at faith in action through Old Testament examples

- Matthew 24:36-51
  Jesus warns us to keep living faithfully

Follow #4

- Matthew 13:1-23
  Following God faithfully leads to growth

- 2 Thessalonians 1
  Persevering through difficulties is evidence of God's work in us

Follow Further Resources

- **Book:** *How to Follow Jesus* by Craig Springer
  An easy-to-read book that takes the mystery out of living a Christian life. A great practical guide for all Christians, including those new to faith.

- **Videos:** *9-a-day Campaign Videos* by Langham Partnership UK
  Excellent, short and simple teaching videos about each fruit of the Spirit and how God grows these in our lives. Christopher J.H. Wright's companion book *Becoming Like Jesus* covers and expands on the same content. Watch the videos on YouTube or at uk.langham.org/get-involved/videos/9-day-campaign-videos

- **Website:** GiftsTest.com by The Rock Church, San Diego
  A helpful resource to find out more about spiritual gifts and think about which gifts God has given to you. Online at giftstest.com/allgifts.

Your Notes

Struggle

The Bible doesn't hide from the reality that life is hard. God doesn't want us to hide our suffering from him either. In an honest friendship with God, we can ask him tough questions and be real about our struggles.

Struggle #1 week beginning _____

Read: Genesis 32:22-32

Jacob was preparing to return home after 20 years away. Because he had left on bad terms with his brother Esau, he was afraid of being attacked when they met. The mysterious struggle in this passage happened after Jacob prayed for God's help with his brother. It ended with God renaming Jacob 'Israel', or 'one who wrestles with God'.

Wrestling may seem like a strange picture for our relationship with God. Some of us might be used to a form of Christianity that is calm and polite, or one that has no room for questions or disagreement. We may have grown up thinking we need to be on our best behaviour with God, or perhaps that it's safest to keep him at arm's length. But wrestling is fierce and messy, up close and personal. It's clinging tightly to your opponent and refusing to let them go.

When we face suffering, confusion or injustice, we have three options. We can either hide our hurt from God, turn our back on him, or wrestle honestly with him. It takes courage to choose the third option. Wrestling with God exercises our faith in his goodness. By voicing our complaint and insisting on God's help, we show that we believe he cares. By clinging to him and refusing to let him go, we come to know him better, and ourselves too. The struggle can be painful and tiring, but as Jacob found, it can also lead to great blessing.

This week, think about how you relate to God when life is hard.

- When you face suffering (your own or other people's), are you more tempted to hide your hurt from God, or to turn your back on him?

- Wrestling is a physical picture. Can you think of a physical picture for your relationship with God?

- Why do you think God wants us to wrestle with him? What does that look like for you?

Your name will no longer be Jacob, but Israel,
because you have struggled with God and
with humans and have overcome.

Genesis 32:28

Weekly Reflections

Good things

Hard things

General mood

How have I wrestled with God?

What help do I need?

What have I worried about?

Who can I ask for help?

What has calmed me down?

Eating	🙂	😐	☹️
Sleep	🙂	😐	☹️
Exercise	🙂	😐	☹️

Prayer for next week

Struggle #2 week beginning _____

> *But Moses sought the favour of the LORD his God ...*
> *Then the LORD relented and did not bring on*
> *his people the disaster he had threatened.*
>
> Exodus 32:11, 14

Read: Exodus 32:1-14

The Israelites had made a golden calf to worship as a visual image of God – something they had been commanded never to do. God was angry, and he told Moses that he had decided to destroy the people and start again. Moses was horrified. He refused to accept this judgment. Instead, he boldly argued with God, begging him to change his mind and forgive the people. And God appeared to do just that!

This passage might seem confusing. The Bible makes it clear that God does not change (Numbers 23:19). But God often acts in creative ways to test us and help us grow. By threatening such a drastic act, God provoked Moses to respond, and to reveal what was in his heart. Moses's strong reaction showed that he loved the people of Israel, and that he knew God did too. Moses cared deeply about God's saving plan for Israel and the world, and he wasn't going to give up on it now.

Moses's passionate arguing actually showed that his heart was lined up with God's.

In the Bible, God has shown us that he is good and loving. But that doesn't mean we always understand what he does. A real friendship with God has space for doubts, questions, complaints and arguments. Like Moses, we can reveal to God whatever is in our hearts, and he will honour our wrestling as genuine faith.

> This week, try to bring your questions and complaints before God.

- Are there things in your life, or in the world, that make you angry, disappointed or frustrated with God?

- How comfortable are you talking to God about these things?

- What else does the Bible say about what God is like? How can knowing these things help you to argue with him like Moses?

But Moses sought the favour of the LORD his God …
Then the LORD relented and did not bring on
his people the disaster he had threatened.

Exodus 32:11, 14

Weekly Reflections

Good things

Hard things

Main focus

How have I brought my doubts or questions to God?

What am I grateful for?

What have I done well?

Who can I thank?

What can I do better?

Eating	☺	😐	☹
Sleep	☺	😐	☹
Exercise	☺	😐	☹

Prayer for next week

Struggle #3 week beginning ‗‗‗‗‗‗‗

> *The Lord … said to Eliphaz … 'I am angry with you …*
> *because you have not spoken the truth about me,*
> *as my servant Job has.'*
>
> Job 42:7

Read: Job 40:6-14, 42:1-9

Job was a good man who lost everything that mattered to him. In despair, he complained to God, and even accused God of attacking him (Job 30:21). His three friends insisted Job must somehow be to blame for his troubles. But when God finally replied to Job, a much bigger picture was revealed.

Beginning to wrestle with God can feel like quite a risk. Since we know that God is perfect and we are not, questioning him at all might just seem wrong. Maybe we are worried that it could be sinful to speak out our frustration with God. Perhaps we feel scared or ashamed of our doubts, and just want to hide them somewhere deep inside us. The first part of this passage might seem to confirm these fears – after all, who are we to question Almighty God? But through Job's wrestling, he came to see God more clearly. In the end, God forgave him for the things he had got wrong, and praised him for his truthfulness. Job's three friends, who had criticised him instead of comforting him, were firmly corrected.

God sees our hearts, whether we voice our feelings or not. It's true that our responses to suffering can be sinful, but burying our pain doesn't make it go away. It's only when we are honest with God about our worst thoughts and fears that he can meet us where we really are, and begin to change us.

> This week, think about the different ways you respond to suffering.

- When you or others are in pain, do you worry that the way you respond might be sinful? Are there things you don't say because of this?

- Do you ever have an urge to criticise people in pain (yourself or others), like Job's friends? Where do you think this comes from?

- What do you think might happen if you voiced your worst thoughts or fears to God?

The Lord … said to Eliphaz … 'I am angry with you …
because you have not spoken the truth about me,
as my servant Job has.'

Job 42:7

Weekly Reflections

Good things

Hard things

General mood

How have I been honest with God?

What do I need to talk about?

How have I blessed others?

Who can I talk with?

How have others blessed me?

Eating	☺	😐	☹
Sleep	☺	😐	☹
Exercise	☺	😐	☹

Prayer for next week

Struggle #4 week beginning _____

> *I pleaded with the Lord to take it away from me.*
> *But he said to me, 'My grace is sufficient for you,*
> *for my power is made perfect in weakness.'*
>
> 2 Corinthians 12:8-9

Read: 2 Corinthians 12:1-10

Paul had heard that there was a group in the Corinthian church who opposed his leadership and were leading other believers astray. So in this letter to them he offered proof after proof of his authority, listing his achievements and clearly showing that God had placed him in this role. Finally in this passage, he talked of his own struggle with God over a 'thorn in the flesh' (v7) that had not been taken away.

Wrestling with God doesn't always get us the answer we want. Sometimes we pray for years without seeing any change, and other times we receive a clear 'no' where we longed for a 'yes'. Jesus himself had this experience when he prayed on the night he was arrested. He begged God to make a way for him to avoid the suffering and death he knew was coming, but instead he was given renewed strength to face it (Luke 22:41-43). Part of the journey of wrestling is to get to a place where, like Jesus and Paul, we can begin to say to God, 'Your will be done', even while the thorn still hurts.

Sometimes in those moments, God gives us precious gifts of understanding that allow us to see more clearly what he is doing in our lives. Paul learned that what he saw as a painful limitation could lead him to rely all the more on God's limitless power. As we ask God to reveal his will for us, we may find wonderful answers we never expected.

> This week, ask God to show you his will in the areas where you are wrestling with him.

- How do you continue bringing your pain to God when it lasts a long time, or when he says 'no' to something you deeply desire?

- How easy is it for you to pray 'Your will be done' to God and mean it? Is there anything that holds you back?

- Has God shown you anything through your suffering that has changed your response to it?

I pleaded with the Lord to take it away from me.
But he said to me, 'My grace is sufficient for you,
for my power is made perfect in weakness.'

2 Corinthians 12:8-9

Weekly Reflections

Good things	Hard things	Main focus

How have I accepted God's will?

What am I proud of?

How have I spoken to myself?

Who can I celebrate with?

What has encouraged me?

	☺	😐	☹
Eating	☺	😐	☹
Sleep	☺	😐	☹
Exercise	☺	😐	☹

Prayer for next week

Struggle Reflections

3-word summary

-
-
-

Verse to remember

What have I found challenging?

What have I found rewarding?

Favourite insight

What will I carry forward?

Struggle prayer

Struggle Optional Extra Bible Passages

Struggle #1

- Habakkuk 1-2

  Habakkuk complains to God about evil in the world

- Mark 7:24-30

  A woman wrestles with Jesus, and gets to know him better

Struggle #3

- Psalm 88

  A psalm that brings every painful feeling to God

- 2 Corinthians 1:3-7

  God comforts us in our pain, and helps us to comfort others

Struggle #2

- Genesis 18:16-33

  Abraham argues with God about the fate of Sodom

- Psalm 44

  A psalm reminding God of his goodness and asking for help

Struggle #4

- Luke 22:39-46

  Jesus wrestles with God

- Romans 8:18-30

  Dealing with suffering and looking forward to future glory

Struggle Further Resources

- **Music:** *Tumbling Sky - Psalms for Weary Souls* by Matt Searles

  A beautiful collection of songs based on psalms that express painful feelings to God. Download for free at mattsearles.bandcamp.com.

- **Video Performance:** *It is Well With My Soul* by the Mormon Tabernacle Choir with Hugh Bonneville

  A moving dramatisation with music and mime. The true story behind Horatio Spafford's famous hymn reveals how the Spaffords' lasting hope in God sustained them through tragedy and loss. Watch on YouTube.

- **Book:** *When Faith Gets Shaken* by Patrick Regan and Liza Hoeksma

  An honest account of Regan's own struggles with God, as well as stories from other Christians. Regan also hosts a series of video interviews about this topic. Watch for free at watch.tbnuk.tv/when-faith-gets-shaken.

Your Notes

Conquer

The Bible tells us that all of creation is caught up in a war between good and evil. The good news is that God has already won the victory! But the battle still goes on, and we have an important part to play.

Conquer #1 week beginning _____

> *Be alert and of sober mind... The devil prowls around... looking for someone to devour. Resist him, standing firm in the faith.*
>
> 1 Peter 5:8-9

Read: 1 Peter 5:1-11

We only have to look around us to know that evil exists. There's no other word strong enough for the most terrible crimes that humans commit. But the Bible tells us that evil doesn't begin with people. It begins with the one who tempted Adam and Eve to turn away from God (Genesis 3:1-7), and who is still doing all he can to pull creation away from its creator. The Bible's names for him are 'Satan' and 'the devil'. These names simply mean 'the enemy' or 'the accuser'.

When God raised Jesus from the dead, he defeated the spiritual powers of evil (Hebrews 2:14-15). Our King has fought for us and won the war! But the battle on the ground is not quite over. Satan will never voluntarily admit defeat. He is determined to keep causing damage. Meanwhile, God and his army of angels are fighting to save as many people as possible from our enemy's clutches before the battle ends (2 Peter 3:9). But because Jesus lives, we can be sure that the battle will end. Then the powers of evil will finally be destroyed, and we will share in God's glorious victory (v4).

The Bible's picture of this spiritual war may be strange and hard to grasp. Some of us may even find it difficult to believe. But as followers of Jesus we need to be aware of the battle going on behind the scenes. Then we can learn how to resist the devil's attacks in our own lives.

This week, celebrate God's victory over Satan, and think about your part in the spiritual battle.

- How do you feel about the idea that there is a spiritual battle going on in the world? Do you feel a part of it?

- What do you know about Satan? What does the Bible say about him?

- How has God's victory over evil changed the world? What changes are we still waiting for?

Be alert and of sober mind ... The devil prowls around ... looking for someone to devour. Resist him, standing firm in the faith.

1 Peter 5:8-9

Weekly Reflections

Good things	Hard things	General mood

When have I been aware of the spiritual battle?

What help do I need?

What have I worried about?

Who can I ask for help?

What has calmed me down?

Eating	☺	😐	☹
Sleep	☺	😐	☹
Exercise	☺	😐	☹

Prayer for next week

Conquer #2 week beginning _____

> *When he [the devil] lies, he speaks his native language,*
> *for he is a liar and the father of lies.*
>
> John 8:44

Read: John 8:31-47

Before going into battle, it's always helpful to understand the enemy's tactics. Our enemy's favourite tactic is simply to lie. Most of his accusations and temptations are rooted in lies about us, about sin or about God. As we learn to spot those lies, we will get better at fighting against them with the truth.

Satan wants to pull us away from God. His goal is to persuade us to attach our hope and identity to anything other than our friendship with the God who made us and loves us. He is a clever con-artist who hides his lies inside false promises, flattery and abuse. He even misuses good things in order to harm us. Our enemy might whisper in our ears that we're better or worse than the people around us. He might try to keep us away from healthy community by telling us we are unwelcome, or tempt us to work too hard by suggesting that our identity is in our performance. He pokes at our deepest needs, fears and flaws, and offers us attractive 'solutions' that are really traps. Jesus knew what he was talking about: he had first-hand experience of Satan's lies (Matthew 4:1-11).

Satan cannot force us to sin. We are all responsible for how we respond to temptation. But it's important to know that he will grab on to anything he can, and use it against us. We must learn how to defend ourselves, and be ready to destroy the devil's lies with the truth, which will set us free (v32).

> This week, try to spot the lies Satan tells you, and fight against them with the truth.

- What are some signs that Satan might be trying to influence your thoughts or actions?

- What are some of the ways you can be pulled away from God and tempted to sin? Can you spot the lies behind them?

- Can you think of any Bible verses or passages that you can remember and use to fight against Satan's lies in your life?

When he [the devil] lies, he speaks his native language,
for he is a liar and the father of lies.

John 8:44

Weekly Reflections

Good things

Hard things

Main focus

How have I fought Satan's lies with the truth?

What am I grateful for?

What have I done well?

Who can I thank?

What can I do better?

Eating	☺	😐	☹
Sleep	☺	😐	☹
Exercise	☺	😐	☹

Prayer for next week

Conquer #3 week beginning _____

> *Finally, be strong in the Lord and in his mighty power.*
> *Put on the full armour of God, so that you can*
> *take your stand against the devil's schemes.*
>
> Ephesians 6:10-11

Read: Ephesians 6:10-20

When he wrote this passage, Paul was thinking of a Roman soldier dressed for battle. Like the soldier, we need to be ready to defend ourselves and fight our enemy. Paul used the soldier's suit of armour as a colourful picture of how we should 'dress' for the spiritual battle we all face every day. Paul's picture of spiritual armour reminds us that our battle is against Satan, not people. It shows us how living a faithful Christian life is our best protection against the enemy's tricks.

First, Paul tells us to fasten God's truth around us like a belt. Second, we should grab hold of Jesus's goodness and wear it across our chests, like a breastplate which defends our hearts against attack. Third, we need to believe and trust in God's saving grace. This gives us a rock-solid helmet to protect our minds when the devil accuses us of being unworthy. Fourth, we must be grounded in the peace that comes from knowing Jesus. Like a strong pair of shoes, this peace will make us ready to do what he asks and go where he calls us. Fifth, our daily choice to keep following and obeying God is like a huge shield. It covers our whole body and stops everything the enemy can throw at us. Sixth, we can use the Bible as a sharp sword to help us fight Satan's lies with words of truth.

Above all, Paul tells us to always pray for help in the battles we face (v18-20). Our mighty God is always fighting for us.

This week, put on your spiritual suit of armour, and ask God for help in the battle.

- If our battle is against Satan, not people, how should we respond to the evil we see in the world?

- Where are the strongest and weakest areas in your spiritual suit of armour?

- Where are the battles in your life? How can you pray for God's help in these?

Finally, be strong in the Lord and in his mighty power.
Put on the full armour of God, so that you can
take your stand against the devil's schemes.

Ephesians 6:10-11

Weekly Reflections

Good things	Hard things	General mood

How have I put on the armour of God?

What do I need to talk about?

How have I blessed others?

Who can I talk with?

How have others blessed me?

Eating	☺	😐	☹
Sleep	☺	😐	☹
Exercise	☺	😐	☹

Prayer for next week

Conquer #4 week beginning _____

> *In all these things we are more than
> conquerors through him who loved us.*
>
> Romans 8:37

Read: Romans 8:31-39

Thinking about the spiritual battle we're in can be unsettling. But the Bible makes one thing very clear: however powerful and cunning our enemy seems to be, he is small and weak compared to God. The good news about Jesus is that he has already defeated sin, death and Satan himself. None of these things, or anything else we may ever come across, can now rip us out of God's mighty hand (v38-39). We are safe, now and for eternity. We are showered with grace and wrapped up in love. And because Jesus has won the victory over Satan, that means we have too! Through Jesus's power we are 'more than conquerors'. We're not just scraping a narrow win. We are crushing the powers of evil under our feet.

In our everyday lives it may not always feel like we are winning. Sin, death and Satan don't seem defeated. They constantly hammer at our door, reminding us that the fight goes on. But the Bible assures us that we crush our enemy every time we resist his lies (James 4:7), every time we choose to do what's right (Romans 12:21) and every time we declare what God has done for us (Revelation 12:10-11).

So we don't need to be afraid. God is on our side (v31)!
We have God's protection, the Holy Spirit's power and the
promise of eternal life. As long as we stay close to our King,
we cannot lose.

This week, remember that you are safe in God's hands.

- How can you stay aware of the spiritual battle without becoming afraid?

- What does it mean for you to be 'more than a conqueror' through Jesus?

- In what ways have you won victories over Satan in your life?

*In all these things we are more than
conquerors through him who loved us.*

Romans 8:37

Weekly Reflections

Good things	Hard things	Main focus

What victories have I won over Satan?

What am I proud of?

How have I spoken to myself?

Who can I celebrate with?

What has encouraged me?

Eating	☺	😐	☹
Sleep	☺	😐	☹
Exercise	☺	😐	☹

Prayer for next week

Conquer Reflections

3-word summary

-
-
-

Verse to remember

What have I found challenging?

What have I found rewarding?

Favourite insight

What will I carry forward?

Conquer prayer

Conquer Optional Extra Bible Passages

Conquer #1

- Daniel 10:1-19
  Daniel receives a glimpse of the unseen spiritual battle

- Revelation 12
  A symbolic picture of Satan's defeat and the ongoing battle

Conquer #2

- Matthew 4:1-11
  Jesus uses the armour of God to resist Satan

- Judges 6 – 7
  God fights a battle for Gideon

Conquer #3

- 2 Corinthians 11:1-15
  Satan deceives us with half-truths and subtle tricks

- James 4:1-10
  Resisting sin and repenting of sin cause the devil to flee

Conquer #4

- Zechariah 9:9-17
  Zechariah prophesies Jesus's victory over evil

- Jude
  Being aware of the spiritual battle without fear as we stay close to God

Conquer Further Resources

- **Video Talks:** *Spiritual Warfare Part One* and *Spiritual Warfare Part Two* by Alistair Begg
  A great introduction to what the Bible teaches about Satan, the spiritual battle and the armour of God. Listen on YouTube or at truthforlife.org/resources/series/grace-and-peace-volume-8/.

- **Book:** *Spiritual Warfare: a biblical and balanced perspective* by Brian Borgman and Rob Ventura
  A more thorough study of each part of the armour of God, and how we can use each of these practically in our everyday lives.

- **Book:** *The Screwtape Letters* by C.S. Lewis
  A satirical book of letters from a fictional demon to his apprentice. A witty and thought-provoking book which cleverly highlights Satan's tactics.

Your Notes

Hope

Because of what Jesus has done for us, we know that death is not the end. We look forward to a wonderful future, where we will live forever with God.

Hope #1

> *Then the saying that is written will come true:*
> *'Death has been swallowed up in victory.'*
>
> 1 Corinthians 15:54

Read: 1 Corinthians 15:16-26, 51-57

Our lives on earth include blessings, challenges, laughter and pain. We can see God's creative work in beautiful landscapes, and sense his kindness in the wonderful moments we enjoy. But we can also see that something has gone wrong in this world that was once 'very good' (Genesis 1:31). Like a rotting apple, everything around us and within us has been infected with sin and death. It's impossible even to fully separate the good from the bad.

People have tried for centuries to fix this mess. But our broken and bruised world can't be patched up by human effort. Only God has the answer. When Jesus died and rose again, his victory was the announcement of a new world to come. There, sin and death will finally be destroyed, and God's goodness and glory will fill all he has created.

The hope that Christians have in Jesus is not just for this life. If it was, as Paul wrote in this passage, it would be no hope at all (v19)! Instead, true hope comes from looking beyond this life, and fixing our eyes on the eternal future that God has promised us (2 Corinthians 4:17-18). In our eternal life, we will fully experience the Jewish idea of 'shalom': peace, wholeness and perfect flourishing. This can only happen in God's presence. We were created to live in friendship with him, and in harmony with all he has made.

> This week, think about the hope we have for eternity.

- What are some differences between the things you hope for in this world and the hope we have in Jesus?

- How much do you think about God's promise of eternal life? Does it affect the way you live?

- How does the idea of 'shalom' shape your understanding of eternal life?

Then the saying that is written will come true:
'Death has been swallowed up in victory.'

1 Corinthians 15:54

Weekly Reflections

Good things

Hard things

General mood

When have I experienced hope for eternity?

What help do I need?

What have I worried about?

Who can I ask for help?

What has calmed me down?

Eating   ☺ ☺ ☹

Sleep   ☺ ☺ ☹

Exercise   ☺ ☺ ☹

Prayer for next week

Hope #2

> *Then I saw 'a new heaven and a new earth,'*
> *...He who was seated on the throne said,*
> *'I am making everything new!'*
>
> Revelation 21:1, 5

Read: Revelation 21:1-14, 22:1-5

There are lots of different ideas about what life after death might be like. Some people imagine clouds and harps, or a kind of non-bodily existence. To some of us, 'heaven' might sound like an eternal holiday, full of luxury and pleasure. But all these ideas are a long way from the Bible's view of eternity, which we can find in the book of Revelation.

Revelation was written by John, one of Jesus's disciples. As an older man, he was given this amazing vision of a new earth, where God would live among his people and rule from his holy city, the new Jerusalem. The images John used can be hard to understand. The things he saw were so wonderful and strange that he had to grasp for familiar things to compare them to, like the city prepared as a bride (21:2) and shining like a jewel (21:11). The river and tree of life (22:1-3) signified a new Garden of Eden (Genesis 2:9) prophesied in Ezekiel 47:12. This is a vision of earth as it was always meant to be – a perfect world, full of God's light and life.

To get closer to a true vision of eternity, we should imagine the world we love, finally released from the evil that infects everything we've ever known. There will be no more death, mourning, crying or pain (21:4). We will see God face to face (1 Corinthians 13:12). Relationships, work and rest will bring us pure joy. And worship will flow through all we do.

> This week, try to imagine the new earth that God has promised.

- Do you have an idea of 'heaven' in your mind? How does it compare to the Bible's vision of eternity?

- Which parts of your life will be transformed in a world released from evil? What might they look like?

- Can you imagine what it will be like to see God face to face? How does this make you feel?

Then I saw 'a new heaven and a new earth,'
…He who was seated on the throne said,
'I am making everything new!'

Revelation 21:1, 5

Weekly Reflections

Good things

Hard things

Main focus

What am I looking forward to in eternity?

What am I grateful for?

What have I done well?

Who can I thank?

What can I do better?

Eating	🙂	😐	☹️
Sleep	🙂	😐	☹️
Exercise	🙂	😐	☹️

Prayer for next week

Hope #3

> *'You have made them to be a kingdom and priests to serve our God, and they will reign on the earth.'*
>
> Revelation 5:10

Read: Revelation 5:6-14

It's an amazing thing to be called God's child. The children of a king have rights and advantages that no one else has. They share his riches. They can come and talk to him any time. And they are his heirs – next in line to rule his kingdom. The Bible says that followers of Jesus are co-heirs with him (Romans 8:17). In the beginning, God gave humans the task of ruling over the earth and looking after it (Genesis 1:26). Instead, we turned away from him, and our world has suffered the effects of sin and death ever since. But when God makes everything new, we will once again live out our true calling. We will rule alongside Jesus over all of creation.

This doesn't mean that our earthly lives don't matter. In fact, the opposite is true, because our task starts here. In our prayers, we ask for God's kingdom to come and his will to be done (Matthew 6:10). As the Holy Spirit works in us, his loving kindness, peace, truth and forgiveness start to trickle into our relationships. And through our words and actions, we bring his light and life into our homes, workplaces and towns.

God has generously shared everything he has with us, his beloved children. Whatever happens to us in this life, our inheritance is secure. And as we faithfully follow Jesus, we are taking the first steps into our future role – paving the way for God's kingdom to transform a world that so badly needs it.

This week, think about how your eternal role affects how you live in the here and now.

- What do you think it will be like to rule alongside Jesus?

- What are some ways you can pave the way for God's kingdom, in your prayers, your life and your relationships?

- If you keep your future role in mind, how might this affect how you see and respond to things in this life?

*'You have made them to be a kingdom and priests
to serve our God, and they will reign on the earth.'*

Revelation 5:10

Weekly Reflections

Good things	Hard things	General mood

How have I paved the way for God's kingdom?

What do I need to talk about?

How have I blessed others?

Who can I talk with?

How have others blessed me?

Eating	☺	😐	☹
Sleep	☺	😐	☹
Exercise	☺	😐	☹

Prayer for next week

Hope #4

> *Since, then, you have been raised with Christ,*
> *set your hearts on things above, where Christ is,*
> *seated at the right hand of God.*
>
> Colossians 3:1

Read: Colossians 1:3-14, 3:1-4

Most of us avoid thinking too much about death. We think and act as if our earthly lives will last forever, and many of us take for granted things like health, safety, relationships and money. But these things can suddenly disappear, and our earthly lives themselves will one day come to an end.

The good news is that our true hope is in 'things above'. We will have troubles in this life, but Jesus's victory over sin and death is a solid foundation, reminding us of our glorious future (John 16:33). The rain will come, and at times we may feel like everything is crashing in on us. But though we might be shaken and bruised by the storms of this life, we will not be destroyed (2 Corinthians 4:8-9).

Fixing our eyes on Jesus in the good times builds up our strength for the moments when we can barely hang on. As we gaze on our Saviour, his coming glory and our eternal hope, the pieces of our lives will begin to rearrange themselves. Peace and joy will come to the foreground. We will give our whole hearts to the things he has asked us to do. Ordinary, everyday blessings will start to speak of God's kindness towards us. And above all, we will learn that his loving presence is always with us, even when it doesn't feel like it. As Jesus said to his disciples in Matthew 28:20, 'Surely I am with you always, to the very end of the age.'

This week, fix your eyes on Jesus and your eternal hope.

- Are there things in your life that you are tempted to take for granted and rely on?

- What are some practical ways you can focus your thoughts on 'things above'?

- How does it affect your outlook on life to know that Jesus is always with you?

*Since, then, you have been raised with Christ,
set your hearts on things above, where Christ is,
seated at the right hand of God.*

Colossians 3:1

Weekly Reflections

Good things	Hard things	Main focus

How have I set my heart on things above?

What am I proud of?

How have I spoken to myself?

Who can I celebrate with?

What has encouraged me?

Eating	☺	😐	☹
Sleep	☺	😐	☹
Exercise	☺	😐	☹

Prayer for next week

Hope Reflections

3-word summary

-
-
-

Verse to remember

What have I found challenging?

What have I found rewarding?

Favourite insight

What will I carry forward?

Hope prayer

Hope Optional Extra Bible Passages

Hope #1

- John 20
  John's account of Jesus's resurrection

- 2 Peter 3
  A call to trust in the promise of a new world and eternal life

Hope #3

- Daniel 7
  A prophetic dream of God's victory and his people's reign

- 2 Timothy 2:1-13
  Living as a follower of Jesus in light of our inheritance

Hope #2

- Ezekiel 47:1-12
  Ezekiel's vision of a river flowing from God's temple

- Isaiah 65:17-25
  Another vision of the new heavens and new earth

Hope #4

- Philippians 3:7-21
  Earthly things don't compare to knowing Jesus

- Hebrews 12:1-3, 18-28
  Keeping a heavenly perspective

Hope Further Resources

- **Book:** *Eternity Changes Everything: how to live now in the light of your future* by Stephen Witmer

  An inspiring look at what the Bible says about eternity, and how it should affect our daily lives as people looking forward to our future with God.

- **Audio Talk:** *Heaven* by Tim Keller

  Keller clearly explains how our future hope prepares us to live for God in the here and now. Listen at gospelinlife.com/downloads/heaven-5931/ or on YouTube.

- **Book:** *Unshakeable Hope: building our lives on the promises of God* by Max Lucado

  Written in a friendly style and illustrated by interesting stories, this book explores God's promises to us, including his promises about eternity.

Your Notes

Final Words

Thank you so much for reading *Refresh*! We hope it has been helpful to you and that you've been encouraged, comforted and strengthened in your faith as you've explored what a healthy life with God can look like. This is our prayer for you:

> *That you, being rooted and established in love, may have power ... to grasp how wide and long and high and deep is the love of Christ, and to know this love that surpasses knowledge – that you may be filled to the measure of all the fullness of God.*
>
> Ephesians 3:17-19

Thanks

We'd like to thank all those who trialled and gave feedback on *Refresh*, including but not limited to: Dave Jordan, Leah Jeffery, Paula Appleby, Chris Witherall, Jemma Taylor, Kathryn Steenkamp, Jenny Edwards, and the members of the Refresh Facebook group.

We're especially grateful to Debs Rackstraw, Leah de Jager, Clare Jordan and Gill Brazier for their help editing early drafts, and to Claire Musters, Natalie Williams, Ruth Alliston, Jonathan Bugden, Stephen Hancock and Graham Holder for their advice on publishing and marketing options.

Our thanks also go to Patrick Regan, Liz Carter, and Steve and Caz Alliston for their kind support and endorsement of the project, and to Malcolm Down, Sarah Grace and their team for seeing the potential in this book and helping us to share it with a greater audience.

Our greatest thanks goes to Jesus our Saviour, who is the ultimate inspiration for this project and our reason for being.

About Us

Jo has worked with disabled clients for fifteen years as a support worker and music therapist. She lives with cystic fibrosis, and has been a Christian since she was thirteen. Jo loves to make the Bible easier for others to understand. Other things that bring her joy include singing and writing songs, pottering in the garden and cuddling Dillon the cat. She also really likes jelly babies.

Dan works in the railway and became a Christian at the age of twenty-seven. He has a passion for capturing the beauty and quirkiness of God's creation and on his days off can often be found on a muddy hill with a camera.

Jo and Dan have been married for six years. They are members at Crawley Community Church, where they help to lead a small group for people with additional learning needs.

You can find more of Jo's writing on our website, **valleyofsprings.com**. You can also follow us on social media at **facebook.com/valleyofsprings** and **instagram.com/valleyofsprings**.